REFRAMING THE CURRICULUM

D1528584

Reframing the Curriculum is a practical, hands-on guide to weaving the concepts of healthy communities, democratic societies, and social justice into academic disciplines. Developed for future and practicing teachers, this volume is perfect for teacher education courses in instructional design, social foundations, and general education, as well as for study in professional learning communities. The author outlines the philosophies, movements, and narratives shaping the future, both in and out of classrooms, and then challenges readers to consider the larger story and respond with curriculum makeovers that engage students in solving problems in their schools, communities, and the larger world. The book's proven method for designing units gives educators across grades and disciplines the tools to bring sustainability and social justice into experiential, project-based instructional approaches.

Pedagogical features include:

- Specific examples and templates that offer readers a framework for reworking their units and courses while meeting required standards and incorporating innovative classroom practices.
- Activities and discussion questions that bring the content to life and establish ties with the curriculum.
- eResources, including a *Facilitator's Guide*, offering examples of fully developed units created with this model and an editable template for redesigning existing units.

Susan Santone is Founder and Executive Director of Creative Change Educational Solutions and an instructor at the University of Michigan's School of Education.

REFRAMING THE CURRICULUM

Design for Social Justice and Sustainability

Susan Santone

KAPPA DELTA PI
INTERNATIONAL HONOR SOCIETY IN EDUCATION
INDIANAPOLIS, INDIANA

KAPPA DELTA PI
INTERNATIONAL HONOR SOCIETY IN EDUCATION

Routledge
Taylor & Francis Group

NEW YORK AND LONDON

First published 2019
by Routledge
711 Third Avenue, New York, NY 10017

and by Routledge
2 Park Square, Milton Park, Abingdon, Oxon, OX14 4RN

Routledge is an imprint of the Taylor & Francis Group, an informa business

Library of Congress Cataloging-in-Publication Data
Names: Santone, Susan, author.
Title: Reframing the curriculum: design for social justice and
sustainability / Susan Santone.
Description: New York, NY: Routledge, 2019. |
Includes bibliographical references and index.
Identifiers: LCCN 2018014237 | ISBN 9781138305960
(hardback: alk. paper) | ISBN 9781138305977 (pbk.: alk. paper) |
ISBN 9780203728680 (ebook)
Subjects: LCSH: Curriculum change. | Social justice—Study and teaching. |
Sustainability—Study and teaching.
Classification: LCC LB1570 .S2844 2019 | DDC 375.006—dc23
LC record available at https://lccn.loc.gov/2018014237

ISBN: 978-1-138-30596-0 (hbk)
ISBN: 978-1-138-30597-7 (pbk)
ISBN: 978-0-203-72868-0 (ebk)

Typeset in Bembo
by codeMantra

Visit the eResources: www.routledge.com/9781138305977

For those who must live tomorrow with the choices we make today.

CONTENTS

ILLUSTRATIONS

Figures

Tables

ABOUT THE AUTHOR

Susan Santone is a passionate educator with more than 20 years of experience in teacher education, curriculum development, school improvement, and educational policy. She is Founder and Executive Director of Creative Change Educational Solutions (http://www.creativechange.net), a nonprofit consulting firm that partners with schools and universities to reorient courses and curriculum around sustainability and social justice. Through Creative Change, she has led national curriculum reform and professional development initiatives with clients ranging from K–12 districts to Big Ten universities to the United Nations. She publishes and consults on sustainability, neoliberalism in education, ecological economics, social justice, and democratic education. She is also an instructor at the University of Michigan School of Education, teaching graduate and undergraduate courses on education reform and multicultural education. As a former instructor at Eastern Michigan University, she taught undergraduate courses on the social/political foundations of education and graduate courses on teaching ecological economics and curriculum design.

PREFACE

Has a book ever changed your life? (No, I'm not suggesting this one will.) Rather, I wanted to tell you about the book that changed my life—and how it ultimately led to the one in your hands.

In 1986, I graduated college with a music education degree. Like a good music student, I holed up and practiced hours each day. After 4 years, I left school with an in-depth knowledge of music, but scant awareness of the world around me.

Then a friend gave me *Food First* by Frances Moore Lappé and Joseph Collins (1977). The book is a sweeping exposé of global hunger and its roots in colonialism. Of all the atrocities, one fact shook me to my core: Food was being *exported* from countries where people were going hungry. What?! The raw injustice consumed me. I didn't understand all the layers, but that didn't matter. This stopped *now*. I was convinced that it would all change if people only understood the problem. And I would be the one to teach them.

That was the beginning of a seismic shift in my life. For the next 10 years, I slogged through a reeducation, both formal and informal. I was obsessed with the challenge of teaching issues like hunger, and I slowly began to incorporate ideas into my various teaching gigs: middle school, English classes for immigrants, cultural immersion programs for exchange students—any setting that gave me the space to develop my own curriculum. I enrolled in graduate school, and for my capstone project, I developed and piloted a high school unit on sustainable agriculture. The program evaluations showed strong gains in content knowledge, critical thinking, and other outcomes in the standards. I was beyond ecstatic. Look what was possible! It was time to spread the word.

A conference workshop—my very first—provided an opportunity. I fully intended to bring down the house, and prepared my data and student work samples. It was game on. I knew that once people saw this work, the ideas would spread, and I'd turn the curriculum world on its head. I delivered the session with bright-eyed gusto, and the participants were indeed interested. Overcome with enthusiasm, I ended the session with a triumphant declaration that curriculum could change the world. (Cue doves.) I waited for the thunderous applause, bracing to be swarmed. But the faces had fallen, and the applause was tepid at best. Then one woman raised her hand and said, "But what am I going to do on Monday?" I was speechless. How could we do anything *but* teach for change? And didn't she see the great results?

But her statement made me face the truth: Teachers aren't held responsible for saving the world; they're held responsible for achievement. And even though the curriculum proved effective, the approach was so profoundly different from commercial materials that few teachers had the time or energy to take it on. I had let idealism eclipse reality, and I realized that quixotic visions cannot be the sole design criteria for curriculum.

But still I faced the curriculum writer's ultimate puzzle: how to turn humanity's three-dimensional enigmas—from food systems to inequalities in the classroom—into culturally relevant, standards-based curriculum distilled for each grade and discipline. But the type of lessons I found—"Have students brainstorm solutions to global problems"—just weren't cutting it. So I dug in and formulated countless curriculum maps, outlines, units, and more. Yet the materials I developed were so dense that students got trapped in investigating problems before ever seeing—let alone developing—solutions. How could I engage and motivate students rather than overwhelm them? It was back to the drawing board. Then I noticed that every structure I created had something in common: a beginning, middle, and ending. And then it hit me: It's a story! (My colleague Shari Saunders witnessed the birth, and I thank her for the unwitting midwifery.)

From that point on, my guiding framework has been *narrative*, a construct both hefty enough to carry the complexity of the world's challenges and familiar enough to make big content accessible for both students and teachers. The concept of narratives also invites us to consider the hidden potential of our curriculum: What if it could help students become literate enough about the world to influence what happens? What if we could advance equity with content that teaches it? The pages ahead will support you to turn these possibilities into reality.

Idealism can fuel your dreams or crush your spirit. For me, it's done both. This book may not change your life, but it will help you make a difference for your students.

Reference

Lappé, F. M., & Collins, J. (1977). *Food first*. New York, NY: Ballantine Books.

ACKNOWLEDGMENTS

It would take another book to properly thank everyone who's inspired and influenced me. Since that's not possible, I'll do my best here.

I've been fortunate to be surrounded by wonderful colleagues, although that is hardly the right word; mentor, supporter, and friend are more like it. My deepest thanks to Lisa Lixey Babe, Jim Crowfoot, June Gorman, Stan Hutton, Lori Kumler, Martha Kaufeldt, Lori Kumler, Ethan Lowenstein, Rebecca Martusewicz, Paul McNamara, Ellen Metzger, Sarah Pounders, Kim Reynolds, Chris Seguin, Trent Stevens, Elissa Trumbull, Lisa Voelker, John Warbach, Khalif Williams, and Mellissa Wilson as well as the many dedicated teachers I've had the honor to work with. Shari Saunders has been a relentless champion and wonderful collaborator. Victor Nolet and Rosalyn McKeown have long been inspirations.

My students are often my best teachers, and these include Annie Delaney, Chandler Lach, Kevin Kollar, and Erik F. Potere. Shane Emery, Robin Peshick, and Evan Caccavelli eased the burden for me in so many ways. David Reynolds stood by my side year after year through every up and down. I am forever grateful. Cliff Jackson has taught me that sustainability and social justice unite both faiths and hearts.

A special thanks to Faye Snodgress, who nurtured the partnership with Kappa Delta Pi that made this book possible. Kathie-Jo Arnoff has been a dream editor, providing the perfect blend of creative freedom and strong direction.

Finally, to my parents: You have been tireless cheerleaders, even when you weren't sure what the game was really about. Your constant love and support enabled me to flourish. This would not have happened without you.

INTRODUCTION

The future is a story yet to be written, and today's students will write tomorrow's chapters. The truth is, we're asking kids to take on some pretty daunting plots at home and abroad: a changing environment, violence, and even equal opportunity in their own classrooms. We're living through an epic, a drama, a tragedy, and a comedy all rolled into one, and putting it all in our students' hands to resolve. Metaphorically, educators are coauthors, and what and how we teach influences where students can take the story. But where is our curriculum leading them? Deeper into the narrative that "things can't change"—or toward a new story of opportunity? Indeed, we must ask ourselves, *How can we create curriculum that provides all students with the educational opportunities they need to author the future they want?*

This book will introduce you to the principles of sustainability, social justice, and educational equity and then guide you, step by step, to create unit or course makeovers based on these ideals. Regardless of grade or discipline, you'll learn how to reframe your curriculum around real-world concerns and develop new ways to improve learning by placing standards in a meaningful context. Most importantly, you'll see how doing so gives students access to the challenging learning opportunities they deserve. Consider these real examples:

- A third-grade teacher in a high-poverty community builds an integrated unit focused on community health. As students gather and communicate data, they gain skills in graphing, reading, speaking, and writing.
- In a predominantly low-income, African-American middle school, a social studies teacher redesigns the history course to emphasize social change and democracy. The engaging content is delivered with intensive literacy instruction, resulting in increased achievement on Common Core literacy and writing skills.

- In a rural Oregon high school, a science teacher develops a course built around the remediation of a contaminated local property. Students investigate environmental issues and present solutions to state leaders, gaining skills in science and civic engagement.

In each case, issues of personal and social significance form layered plots that students must resolve with positive solutions. But even if your disciplines are not issue-oriented, you'll discover many opportunities to reframe your curriculum using concepts such as well-being and interdependence. For example,

- Using the concept of well-being, a physical education teacher helped his students challenge bullying and gender-based stereotyping based on athletic ability and body image.
- A middle school Spanish teacher applied the concept of interdependence to verb conjugations, and students used the command forms to lead each other through the school's nature trail.

Over the past 20+ years, I've been fortunate to work alongside talented teachers who have proven again and again that we don't have to choose between standards and creative, dynamic teaching; you'll see this in examples throughout the book. Indeed, your redesigned curriculum will likely exceed standards because the meaningful challenges you embed *require* that students master the material. That said, this approach is a paradigm shift for educators used to (or forced to) teaching stand-alone lessons based on a checklist of standards.

How we relate to students is just as much a part of the learning experience as the content. That's why this book addresses two layers of curriculum: (a) the *explicit* curriculum of units, courses, syllabi, textbooks; and (b) the *hidden* curriculum of school climate, relationships, and expectations. You'll learn how the explicit and implicit curricula inform each other, and how we can adapt both to improve learning outcomes.

Who Should Read This Book?

Teacher educators, preservice teachers, practicing K–12 teachers, and university instructors will find tools and solutions to meet their needs and goals:

- Curriculum and methods instructors (and their students) will gain strategies to teach standards through the principles of sustainability and social justice.
- Social foundations instructors and students will learn ways to bridge theory and practice.
- K–12 teachers across disciplines will learn practical strategies to energize their teaching as well as a unique approach to project-based learning.

- International Baccalaureate (IB) educators will find approaches that (in one teacher's words) "bring the IB framework to life" with rigorous, interdisciplinary units.
- Curriculum directors will gain a new perspective on curriculum as a whole, supported by a redesign approach that can be implemented through in-house professional development.
- University instructors from any discipline who are seeking to integrate sustainability across the curriculum will find both the theoretical foundations and a well-tested process for instructional design.

What's Inside?

Reframing curriculum based on the principles of sustainability and social justice requires seeing your discipline and indeed, society at large, in a new way. You'll need to understand the parallels between, for example, economic inequality in society and deficit thinking in the classroom, or social-environmental interdependence and place-based education. The book's three-part structure will provide both the necessary theory and practical applications.

Part I, "What's at Stake?," will deepen your understanding of sustainability and social justice to provide context for our work as educators. Chapter 1 provides an overview of trends shaping the future, both in and out of classrooms. Chapter 2 examines the narrative of competitive individualism and economic growth that dominates the world today, and Chapter 3 presents an alternative narrative based on thriving communities, shared prosperity, social equity, and environment health. As you compare the paradigms, you'll vividly see the root beliefs and assumptions that drive the way things are as well as the way they could be. You'll formally define *sustainability* and *social justice* in the Part I Culminating Activity.

Part II, "What's at Stake in Our Curriculum?," examines how the competing narratives play out in curriculum and classroom practice. Chapter 4 introduces the pedagogical principles of teaching for sustainability and social justice, including democratic education, and culturally responsive teaching. Chapter 5 exposes the ways education can reinforce unsustainability and inequality, with clear guidance on what not to do. Returning to the Story We Want, Chapter 6 builds on Chapter 4 by providing specific teaching strategies applicable across grades and disciplines. In the "Part II Culminating Activity," you'll apply what you've learned to assess your own unit or course using rubrics provided on the book's website.

With this foundation, you'll take on curriculum (re)design in Part III, "Changing the Story: Curriculum Design With the Stakes in Mind." Each of the four chapters brings you through a distinct step of a process designed to unleash your creativity. In Chapter 7, you'll (re)define the big-picture focus for your unit, and in Chapter 8, you'll develop guiding questions. Chapter 9 focuses on learning outcomes, and Chapter 10 brings it all together as you align standards, instruction, and assessment. Again, the website provides a rubric to evaluate your work.

Ways to Use This Book

Adopting new ways of teaching takes time, and that's why this book is best used in a facilitated environment such as a teacher education course or an extended curriculum redesign initiative. A *Facilitator's Guide*, available on the book's website, offers strategies for using the book in different contexts. But before you access that, here are some basic guidelines: First, it is important to read the chapters in order. Skipping ahead to the curriculum design process in Part III will be less effective and even confusing without the content and pedagogies presented across Parts I and II. Second, whether you are using this book in a facilitated setting or reading it as an individual, take time to complete the activities and questions throughout the book, as they're designed to help you hit the ground running in Part III.

Book Features

The following tools will support you to master both the theory and practical applications:

- Activities and discussion questions in each chapter will bring the content to life and establish ties with your curriculum.
- Ample frameworks and matrices (with additional tools on the book's website) show how the ideas apply across grades and disciplines.
- As noted, the *Facilitator's Guide*, also available online, outlines how to use specific sections of the book for individual course sessions or workshops. Teacher educators will also find suggestions for pairing the book with additional readings.
- The book's website offers a fully developed unit designed with the approach presented in the book. An editable template to guide the design of your unit is also provided.

It's democratic, Not Democratic

Maybe you're getting excited about the chapters ahead, but a little voice says, "If we do all this work, aren't we just indoctrinating students? What if I arouse suspicion or get parents angry? What if someone labels me a 'Commie'?"

This book refutes the idea that teaching through an equity lens is political. Equal opportunity is not a controversial issue; it's in the Constitution. Educators must advocate for equity; to do otherwise condones indifference to injustice. "Silence is political," a student wisely observed. As you'll learn, our job is to establish democratic ideals and help students use them as a lens for decision-making. Granted, it can be confusing to differentiate between advocacy and editorializing, but the distinction is critical: The former is our professional obligation; the latter squelches critical thinking. Let me share an example.

On Wednesday, November 9, 2017 at 9 a.m.—just hours after the election of Donald Trump—I walked into my Social Foundations class to find most of my students, including three Muslims, looking shell-shocked. One student, a White female, shrugged and said, "I voted for him."

I neither took a side nor shared how I voted; spouting my views would not have sharpened my students' critical thinking skills. However, I did not ignore the election on the belief that I must be *neutral*. Instead, I emphasized our professional responsibility to consider the administration's potential impacts on equity, the common good, human dignity, and the well-being of children— topics we'd been studying for 2 months. While I clearly took a stand, it was for our obligation to advocate for equal opportunity.

Everyone loses when standing up for justice is demonized as a radical agenda. This distortion dissolves what should unite us: the realization that equity (a "liberal" goal) enables individual initiative (a "conservative" virtue). There's nothing controversial about helping all students reach their potential.

If you teach in a predominantly White and/or upper-class setting, you may wonder whether the social justice dimensions apply to you. The answer is *absolutely yes!* Here's why: Informed civic engagement is everyone's responsibility. An all-White district that doesn't recognize Martin Luther King Day because "it's not our issue" deprives students from learning about the evolution of our common democracy. And as we'll discover, there are psychological implications to turning our backs on community.

I wrote this book because I believe in the power of curriculum to broaden minds, open hearts, and lift up communities. Yet too often, mandates pull teachers and students out of authentic environments, plunk them into a cardboard setting, and hold them accountable to a story they had no role in making. The tensions between what we want to teach and what we have to teach can seem insurmountable. You're about to learn how to bridge the chasm. And when you turn the final page, you'll have new ways to prepare your students to shape the world they want.

Fasten your seat belt and let's get started.

PART I
What's at Stake?

1

WHAT'S THE STORY WE WANT?

As of this writing, the twenty-first century is almost 20% behind us. And when we consider that a child born today may live to see the year 2100, "21st century learning" seems downright inadequate as the blueprint to prepare students. Isn't it time we considered educating for the twenty-second century? This chapter will orient us to the path ahead.

Given our context is sustainability and social justice, you can just about guarantee that you're in for a sobering account of the world's problems: climate change, racial inequality, violence … the list, unfortunately, goes on. You'll hear some of those troubles in the pages to come—intellectual honesty demands it—but simply asking, *What's wrong with the world?* sets us up for apathy. A litany of woes can weigh us down so hard that it becomes impossible to look up and imagine a way out. That's why I'll start our journey with a different question: *What's the story we want for ourselves, our students, and our communities, near and far?*

In workshops and courses over the past 22 years, I've posed this question to people of all ages and backgrounds: children, preservice educators, inservice teachers, college professors and administrators, self-identified "conservatives" and "progressives," veterans, Catholic nuns, and other people of faith. Sometimes I use one of these variations:

- What do we need for a fulfilling life?
- What do we need to be happy and healthy?
- What does it take to thrive as individuals and communities?

Regardless of the wording or audience, the answers have been remarkably the same. Before I reveal them, take a moment and respond yourself. Tip: Try organizing your responses by category, such as physical needs, social needs, economic needs, among others.

All done? Here are the responses I hear every (and I mean *every*) time. Drumroll, please.

- Clean water and air;
- Healthy, affordable foods appropriate to cultures and communities;
- Health care;
- Supportive and loving relationships: family, friends, neighbors;
- Educational opportunities: schools, books, Internet, informal learning;
- Economic opportunities: jobs, access to financing;
- Transportation, energy, infrastructure;
- Fair governance structures; and
- Recreation and self-expression: hobbies, art, music, sports, etc.

This list reflects common "ingredients" essential to a fulfilling life (Ben-Shahar, 2007). While I've heard these responses countless times, I never tire of seeing people light up when—often for the first time—they speak about what they want, not what they fear, avoid, or lament. And when I ask a related question—*What do we want for our students?*—the responses again are strikingly similar: high-quality learning and opportunities for LL student A to become well-rounded people, involved citizens, and contributing members of society. The conversation expands, and we consider whether the goals apply across places, cultures, and generations. The answer has been an overwhelming *yes,* albeit with variations. For example, some participants raise the fact that education must adapt to the local context, while others point out that definitions of beauty are culturally determined. Absolutely. Through these discussions, participants acknowledge that, while specifics can and should vary, the desire to thrive is widely shared and (as some participants say) a "timeless" goal.

Here's the punch line: I have yet to meet anyone who does not want strong families, healthy communities, and students who fulfill their potential. But it's this very universality that calls out the elephant in the room: Who is responsible for the provision of healthy foods, safe housing, education, and other "ingredients" of thriving? Are they a social right, or are individuals responsible for acquiring them through their own efforts? Is it a combination of both? This eternal debate requires extended inquiry; however, I raise it now because I've found that no matter where people fall on the issue, they tend to agree on a basic premise: Everyone should at least have a fair shot in life. Even firm advocates of individual responsibility acknowledge that the proverbial "level playing field" is a central value of our democracy. In this way, we establish fairness and opportunity as conditions for thriving.

The vision and values I hear again and again are hardly anecdotal; indeed, they are articulated at the global level through the Earth Charter (EC), an "international declaration of fundamental values and principles for building a just, sustainable, and peaceful global society" (Earth Charter Initiative, 2016). The EC began taking shape before the 1992 Rio Earth Summit, and after a decade of global-level consensus building, the EC was launched in 2000. Underscoring the "great peril and great promise" of the future (Preamble), the EC is built upon four pillars: Respect and Care for the Community of Life; Ecological Integrity; Social and Economic Justice; and Democracy, Nonviolence and Peace. The EC Initiative continues today through education and community-level actions.

Before we get all Pollyanna, let's be clear that we can't rest on a vision, bring it in for a hug, and call it a day. Far too many individuals, schools, and communities are not thriving, and we must determine *how* to change this and define our ethical obligations as educators. There's no feel-good consensus for that. But imagining a happier story better positions us for success than simply wringing our hands. Articulating a vision is inherently motivating because it illuminates a destination and holds up the goals worth striving for. It also prompts us to celebrate progress we're already making, whether it's better achievement or a stronger local economy. This mindset enables us to say, "Yes, there are problems, but there are also solutions—and some are happening now."

Is this idealistic? Yes (and I've shared the pitfalls of that). But we are failing our students if our curriculum sends the message that the problems are too big and it's pointless to try. We don't want the takeaway to be, "Forget about thriving, kids. The best we can hope for is to simply survive." That's not the stuff of schoolwide themes.

With this framing (and perhaps your own goals defined), here are questions we'll explore throughout the rest of this chapter:

- What supports thriving and well-being?
- Where are the major plots, in and out of schools? Where is the story headed?
- Who's benefiting? Who's bearing the burdens?
- How is it all connected?

These are big questions with big answers, so let's get started.

What Supports Thriving and Well-Being?

Let's start with an activity. Review Table 1.1, noting the difference between the items in Groups A and B. If you said that Group A items are from nature and that those in Group B are human-created, you are correct.

TABLE 1.1 What Supports Our Well-Being?

Group A	Group B
Sunlight	Local history
Rivers	Community celebrations
Oxygen	Libraries
Insects	Language
Soil	Dialects
Forests	Songs
Bacteria	Poems
Genes	Parks
DNA	Education
Rocks	Roads
Ores	Sewers
Hills	The power grid
Sunsets	Public markets
Oceans	The Internet

The Commons

Together, the elements in the table are examples of the "Commons," the shared ecological and cultural gifts that support well-being (Rowe, 2013). The ecological/environmental Commons include oxygen, water, sunlight, and other things that sustain life for humans and "more-than-human" beings (Martusewicz, Edmundson, & Lupinacci, 2011, p. 86). The human-created, social/cultural Commons include roads, public education, language, and other elements that contribute to community well-being, locally to globally. Again, this varies by culture; not everyone relies on sewers or formal schooling, for example.

Defining the Commons reveals another important reality: We not only have shared goals, but we share the essentials needed to reach those goals. Explore this more in Activity 1.1.

Activity 1.1. Explore the Commons

1. Review the two lists again. What else would you add to each? What other Commons contribute to our well-being? (We'll use "Commons" as a singular noun, e.g., the sun is a Commons.)
2. Are there items from either list that aren't needed to thrive? Consider how your answers may vary based on individual needs, cultures, community, or time frame.
3. Choose at least one term from each list and describe how they work together to support well-being. Examples: oceans and sunsets (from Group A)

can inspire songs and poems (from Group B). Generate as many connections as you can. (Optional: Write each word on a separate sticky note or file card; use a different color for each list if possible. Then arrange the individual items into clusters or webs to show the connections.)
4. After you've generated your connections, remove a few items from your cluster. For example, if you connected sunlight, soil, roads, and public markets, toss out soil or roads. What happens to the rest of the cluster?
5. Bring it outside: Take a quick tour around your campus or neighborhood. What are examples of ecological and cultural Commons? How do they work together?

Interdependence

The relationships among the Commons as uncovered earlier illustrate our next concept: interdependence. Our well-being depends on healthy relationships between ecological and social systems. Humans are animals, and we are every much a part of the environment as the polar bear. And while we might not recognize it (yet), everything humans make takes materials out of the environment and puts wastes back into it. This is not a tree-hugger view of the world: It's the ironclad laws of nature, as we'll explore later. As you can see, humans are not the only species that matter. If we are to thrive, so must everything else. Going forward then, our definition of "community" will include not only people but also the elements and relationships innate to the Commons. We will study what's really there: connections and systems, not merely components that exist independently (Meadows, 2008).

Understanding the basics of the Commons equips us to tackle a more layered question: To what extent is the way we're doing things moving us toward the Story We Want *while also* sustaining the shared ecological and cultural gifts the story depends on? This is the yardstick we'll apply to assess whether we're headed in the right direction. With this tool in hand, let's think about some of the "plots" unfolding in the world today.

Where Are Major Plots In and Out of Schools? Where Is the Story Headed?

To put the present in perspective, let's take a quick look back to a historical turning point that launched the "modern" world of today: the Industrial Revolution (about 1760). Industrialization introduced profound social and economic changes: the advent of large-scale manufacturing and agriculture; sweeping medical advances; cars, planes, refrigeration, and other technologies that reshaped everyday life. This industrialization paralleled dramatic improvements in global life span, literacy rates, and more. Over the same time frame, the global human population swelled from 1 billion to 7.5 billion.

Before we conclude that industrialization inevitably improves well-being for all, let's remember that this transition and its modern manifestation (globalization) have left many people behind. Moreover, these changes have been fueled by ever-expanding mining, drilling, and deforestation—an "extractive economy" that has degraded the ecological systems it depends on (Hornborg, McNeill, & Martinez-Alier, 2007). Because it's impossible to separate the economy from human well-being and the environment, we'll keep them all in mind as we assess global trends.

The United Nations 2015 Sustainable Development Goals (SDGs) are arguably the most comprehensive set of measurable indicators to assess the "state of the world." The 17 goals address environmental quality, energy, gender rights, poverty, health, water and food, and more—categories applicable at the national and local levels as well. (You'll have the opportunity to assess trends in your own community later in this chapter.) Education is highlighted in SDG 4: "ensur[ing] inclusive and quality education and promot[ing] lifelong learning for all." The focus is both participation (91% of children worldwide attend primary school, yet 263 million do not) and global disparities in learning outcomes based on socioeconomic status—a prominent problem in the United States as we'll see.

While all SDG data are readily available online, let's assess where the world stands in three categories: food security, water, and climate change. We'll take a specific look at education later in the chapter.

Food Security

The Food and Agriculture Organization of the United Nations (FAO, 2015) defined food security as "all people, at all times, hav[ing] physical and economic access to sufficient, safe and nutritious food that meets their dietary needs and food preferences for an active and healthy life" (p. 53).[1] Here, the statistics paint a mixed picture. On one hand, the world produces the equivalent of 2,940 calories per capita (FAO, 2015), and the percentage of hungry people in the world has declined from 15% in 2000 to 11% in 2016 (United Nations Economic and Social Council, 2016). On the other hand, one-third of the world's croplands are used to produce food for livestock (FAO, 2012) and an estimated 795 million people are still chronically undernourished, including more than 90 million children (United Nations [UN], 2016). In yet another plot twist, the number of overweight people in the world has surpassed the number of underweight people (Non-Communicable Diseases Risk Factor Collaboration, 2016); in the United States, an estimated 36.5% of adults are obese (Ogden, Carroll, Fryar, & Flegal, 2015).

One factor (at least in the United States) is access to healthy and affordable foods. Full-service grocery stores are less prevalent in low-income communities, where residents are more reliant upon on "junk food" from gas stations or convenience stores (U.S. Department of Agriculture Economic Research Service, 2017). Such "food deserts" create conditions for becoming overweight yet undernourished. Farmers markets are a powerful tool to change this. Across the United States, the number of farmers markets is not only surging, but more are also accepting Supplemental Nutrition Assistance Program (SNAP) benefits ("food stamps"; U.S. Department of Agriculture, 2017). Such changes help put healthier foods within reach.

Water

Clean water is another life essential, and here, too, we see mixed trends. At the global level, the United Nations (2016) reported that 2.6 billion people gained access to improved (i.e., potable) drinking water sources between 1990 and 2015. However, 40% of the global population experiences water scarcity—a percentage that is expected to grow as climate change intensifies droughts.

While we might think that drinking water quality is only a problem in "developing" countries, it's also been front-page news in the United States. For example, alleged governmental negligence exposed an estimated 100,000 people to lead in Flint, Michigan from 2014 to 2017; at least five state officials have been charged with involuntary manslaughter (Atkinson & Davey, 2017). In 2016, the city of Detroit cut off water to 23,300 households with delinquent accounts, including many families in rental properties whose landlords failed to pay the bill (Kurth, 2016). The United Nations, which considers water a human right, denounced the city's actions, and community activists rallied to keep the water flowing while bills were being settled (United Nations News Centre, 2016).

Climate Change

The quality and quantity of food and water is affected by climate change, a prominent international concern that knows no boundaries. One key indicator is the amount of carbon in the atmosphere, measured in parts per million (ppm). By 2012, carbon levels were 40% higher than at the start of the Industrial Revolution (National Academy of Sciences, 2014). We've now topped 400 ppm, well over the "safe" target of 350 ppm, a level that scientists believe could avert cataclysmic changes in temperature and precipitation patterns (Hansen et al., 2013).

Climate change is also affecting the oceans—a major carbon sink—in at least two ways: First, oceans will rise, potentially between 0.5 and 1 m (1.5 and 3 ft), by the year 2100 if current trends continue. Second, oceans have absorbed about 30% of the emitted anthropogenic (human-produced) carbon dioxide, changing the water chemistry and causing acidification. This is undermining the health of (among other things) coral reefs, which will negatively impact related fisheries, tourism, and local economies (Hoegh-Guldberg et al., 2007).

The combustion of fossil fuels is a major culprit in climate change, requiring a global transition to renewable energy. Here, there are promising trends. Worldwide, the amount of energy produced by renewable sources—as well as investments in these sources—is at an all-time high (Renewable Energy Policy Network for the 21st Century, 2016). At the 2015 United Nations Conference on Climate Change in Paris, 195 nations committed to carbon reduction actions aimed at limiting temperature increases to below 2 degrees Celsius (UN, 2016). This is all encouraging, yet the question remains: Can the transition keep pace with the world's ravenous energy consumption, projected to increase 56% by 2040 from the 2010 levels (U.S. Energy Information Administration, 2016)?

Who's Benefiting? Who's Bearing the Burdens?

The quality of our food, the cleanliness of our water, and the health of our environment affect everyone—but in very different ways. Some individuals and communities have the benefit of food security and health care, while others bear the burdens of malnutrition and disease. Moreover, the impacts too often correlate with race, socioeconomic status, gender, ethnicity, or age. Clearly, our shared reliance is not translating into shared benefits. This brings us to our next topic.

Equality and Equity

The question of benefits and burdens introduces us to two foundational concepts: equity and equality. While the two terms are often used interchangeably, they have distinct (and sometimes contested) meanings. Let's examine a few definitions.

The terms equal and equality both refer to sameness; for example, equal rights = the same rights. At the global level, the United Nations Development Programme (UNDP, 2011) defined *in*equality as differences and disparities among (or within) populations. In contrast, equity refers to equal opportunity, introducing the "moral dimension" of fairness (Melamed & Samman, 2013, p. 2). For example, the underrepresentation of women in governmental leadership positions is an example of gender inequality (a disparity between men and women). But this inequality is created by gender inequity: women's lack of access to the education, rights, and opportunities that lead to such positions. As the UNDP (2011) stated, "Inequalities in outcomes are largely the product of unequal access" (p. 19).

In terms of income, inequality has reached grotesque levels: The richest 10% of people earn up to 40% of the global total (UN, 2016). The United States has one of the highest levels of income inequality in the world (Organisation for Economic Co-operation and Development, 2017), with one in five children living below the poverty threshold. In terms of education, the correlation be-tween poverty and achievement is well-documented. We'll do a deep dive into this in Part II.

Trauma

Children in poverty are more likely to face burdens in the form of chronic abuse, neglect, economic instability, inadequate health care, exposure to violence—stress factors collectively known as trauma or adverse childhood experiences (ACEs; Centers for Disease Control and Prevention [CDC], 2016). Accord-ing to the CDC, 46% of children in the United States have experienced at least one ACE, and 1 in 10 has experienced three or more. Ongoing expo-sure to high levels of ACEs activates an extended "fight or flight" response that can impact self-regulation, cognitive functioning, and other aspects of brain development (Shonkoff, Boyce, & McEwen, 2009). The condition, known as toxic stress, correlates with adverse outcomes as adults, such as fi-nancial instability, criminal activity, and chronic health problems (Shonkoff et al., 2012).

Research also suggests that trauma has an epigenetic quality, meaning it can influence the expression of genes being transmitted across generations (Bombay, Matheson, & Anisman, 2009, 2014; McGowan & Szyf, 2010). For example, generations of U.S. Native American and Canadian Aboriginal children were forcibly removed from their homes and sent to boarding schools designed to eradicate their cultures (Spring, 2016). In studying intergenerational health in these families, Bombay et al. (2014) reported that the emotional stress from the experiences may have suppressed "the expression of certain genes, which, if present in sperm or ova … could potentially be transmitted from one genera-tion to the next" (p. 332). Trauma thus has implications for intergenerational equity.

Mental health problems also stem from environmental degradation. A 2017 report from the American Psychological Association (Clayton, Manning, Krygsman, & Speiser, 2017) described how the "unrelenting day-by-day de-spair" (p. 27) caused by droughts, storms, and migration can surface as anxiety and depression. Such "ecophobia" (Sobel, 1996) can push people into a state of hopelessness that makes it unlikely to even imagine change.

The corrosive impacts of psychological stressors point to the importance of social-emotional learning and trauma-informed practices, topics we'll revisit throughout the book.

Equality, Equity, and the Environment

Race, ethnicity, geography, or income should not determine the quality of your local environment—yet too often they do. Demographics and the environment intersect through the concept of environmental justice (EJ), the "fair treatment and meaningful involvement of all people regardless of race, color, national origin, or income with respect to the development, implementation, and enforcement of environmental laws, regulations, and policies" (U.S. Environmental Protection Agency [EPA], n.d.). EJ asks, "Are some communities disproportionately exposed to, for example, pollution or contaminated water?" When it comes to climate change, the answer is yes, because the location and demographics of a community can predict the severity of impacts.

For example, warmer temperatures and melting permafrost are destabilizing roads and buildings in the Arctic—a region where infrastructure is already precarious (Nunavut Climate Change Centre, n.d.). Changing weather patterns affect animal populations, upending traditional hunting practices and the cultural knowledge communities have relied on for centuries. Moving south, less-industrialized regions are particularly vulnerable to upheaval given other pressures such as population growth, fragile ecosystems, and economic dependence on agriculture (Kasperson & Kasperson, 2001). Syria provides an example: From 2006 to 2011, a severe multiyear drought crippled agricultural output, leading to population displacements and, eventually, civil unrest. In short, the environmental stresses of climate change will aggravate existing problems and create more instability—a reality the Department of Defense (DoD) sees as an international security issue. In a report to Congress, the DoD (2015) stated,

> DoD recognizes the reality of climate change and the significant risk it poses to United States interests globally. The National Security Strategy, issued in February 2015, is clear that climate change is an urgent and growing threat to our national security, contributing to increased natural disasters, refugee flows, and conflicts over basic resources such as food and water. These impacts are already occurring, and the scope, scale, and intensity of these impacts are projected to increase over time.
>
> (*p. 3*)

In terms of climate change in the United States, geography and demographics again matter. Low-income urban areas often lack the tree canopies and green spaces that provide a cooling effect, exposing residents (especially those without air conditioning) to health risks from heat waves (Stone, Hess, & Frumkin, 2010). Moreover, decades of urban disinvestment and "White flight"— incentivized by federal policies—have left many cities and communities of color unable to invest in adaptations that can increase resiliency, such as improved stormwater management systems (Newman, Beatley, & Boyer, 2009). Aging, inadequate infrastructure leaves such communities more vulnerable to destruction from extreme weather events; Hurricane Katrina is the poster child. These inequities continue a long-standing pattern in which low-income and communities of color are far more likely to be exposed to environmental hazards and less likely to have a voice in shaping related policies (Bullard, 2005; U.S. EPA, n.d.).

Equality and Equity in the Commons of Public Education

In the United States, public schools have long been the cornerstone institution to meet the shared need for education. Today, public schools serve 50 million children from all backgrounds. Publicly funded, community-governed, and open to all, schools are a shining example of a social Commons offering opportunity to everyone.

At least that's the theory. Let's see how it looks through the lens of equality and equity.

In an educational context, *equality* means "sameness" (e.g., equal funding means the same dollars). "Equality" sounds good, but it's a word that's been wielded in ways that support profoundly unfair practices. The infamous concept of "separate but equal" was based on the premise that schools could be segregated but of the same quality. Of course, separate was never equal, as brought to light by the 1954 Supreme Court case, *Brown v. Board of Education* of Topeka. In a unanimous decision, the court struck down racial segregation in schools as "inherently unequal" and a violation of the Fourteenth Amendment. The landmark case cut through the rhetoric of "sameness" and turned attention to fairness, that is, equity—whether every child is provided with access to opportunities to succeed.

The question of equity persists, especially when we consider demographic changes in public schools. In 2014, the K–12 population crossed a major threshold: For the first time, students of color and those from low-income households[2] comprised over 50% of students, and just over 9% are English Language Learners (Maxwell, 2014; National Center for Education Statistics [NCES], 2016a). And while *Brown v. Board* outlawed racial segregation, a string of subsequent Supreme Court rulings since then have eased compliance requirements for integration, resulting in levels of segregation now rivaling those of the Civil Rights era (Coleman et al., 1965; NCES, 2016a; Reardon & Owens, 2014).

Segregation is also increasing along socioeconomic lines, evidenced by a growing number of high-poverty schools—those in which 75% or more of children are eligible for free or reduced lunch. Between 2006 and 2013, the number of students in high-poverty school districts increased from 15.9 million to 24 million (Brown, 2015). Here, race and class intersect: Students of color are more likely to be concentrated in high-poverty districts. In the 2012–2013 school year, 45% of Black and Hispanic students, but only 8% of White students, attended such schools (Kena et al., 2015). There is also an EJ dimension; these schools—like their surrounding communities—are more likely to be located near polluted areas or have unhealthy conditions such as mold and poor indoor air quality (Fischbach, 2005).

In the land where education is the great equalizer, race, class, and zip code should have no bearing on educational quality. But across the board—from test scores to graduation rates—the outcomes of Black, Latino, Native American, and low-income students lag behind their White, wealthier peers. For some indicators, such as reading scores, disparities based on socioeconomic status now eclipse those based on race (NCES, 2016a; Reardon, 2011). While there's been some improvement in recent years—an uptick in high school graduation rates and a gradual narrowing of racial/ethnic gaps in math and reading (National Assessment of Educational Progress [NAEP], 2018; NCES, 2016a)—the data in Table 1.2 show that we have not come far enough.

These disparities are often lumped together as the *achievement gap,* that is, unequal outcomes. But we will focus on the root culprit: the *opportunity gap*—unequal access to the conditions and resources needed for success. Public education, a pillar of the social Commons, is not equitably serving all. The need for quality education is shared, but access to it is not.

TABLE 1.2 Snapshot of Educational Outcomes by Race and Socioeconomic Status

	Reading scores, Grade 4	Reading scores, Grade 8	Math scores, Grade 4	Math scores, Grade 8	High school dropout rates	College attendance rates	College completion rates
White	231	274	248	292	4.4%	42%	43.7%
Black	205	248	223	260	6.2%	33%	21.4%
Hispanic	208	255	229	268	7.3%	35%	30.4%
Asian*	n/a	n/a	n/a	n/a	1.5%	63%	47.7%
Pacific Islander*	n/a	n/a	n/a	n/a	5.1%	24%	26.7%
Asian and Pacific Islander	239	280	257	306	n/a	n/a	n/a
American Indian/ Alaskan native	205	252	227	267	12.5%	23%	23%
Low poverty	241	281	257	301	2.4%	83.6%	60%
High poverty	205	248	226	264	9.9%	57.8%	14%

NAEP (2018); NCES (2014, 2015a, 2015b, 2015c, 2016b, 2016c, 2016d, 2016e)
★ Separate data for Asian and Pacific Islander not available in some cases.

How Is It All Connected?

We've covered wildly divergent topics from carbon emissions to graduation rates. Yet these seemingly unrelated issues are symptoms of the same malady: the broken bonds between social and ecological communities. We are failing to sustain a healthy Commons, and it is failing to sustain us in equitable ways.

None of these problems can be contained in neat boxes or stopped at the border. We're all actors on a shared stage, and even if we enact separate plots in our own corners, eventually, my story will spill into yours—or perhaps it did long ago, and I'm just now realizing it. This speaks to the nature of the wicked problems before us: They are systemic, lack clear solutions, and span time and place (Brown, Harris, & Russell, 2010; Nolet, 2015).

The bad news here is that it's all connected. But that's also the good news. If the problems stem from damaged and dysfunctional relationships, we can flip the script and restore healthier ways of interacting among people, communities, and the environment. If food desserts contribute to poor health, we can start changing the story through community gardens. If trauma impairs students' ability to learn, we can begin to create compassionate and nurturing classrooms. And while challenges such as climate change require long-term global action, we can here and now be, for example, reducing energy use in our homes and schools. Every action is a step toward the Story We Want, and millions of people are marching in the same direction. In researching the scale of global efforts, Hawken (2007) posited that more than 1,000,000 organizations are working to advance environmental protection, social justice, and more. Your own work is no doubt a part of this.

Where is your own community headed? The *Facilitator's Guide* on the book's website offers activities to explore this.

Because we all rely on the Commons, it's tempting to imagine a Utopian setting to our story where everything is limitless and free. But we know that's not how it works.

One factor is cost. Providing nutritious food, clean water, and education takes resources, whether public or private. We pay for clean water through individual and collective means (e.g., a utility bill or taxes). Attending public school is free to the individual but requires public expenditures. Even people who gather their own water, grow their own food, or pitch in with neighbors to build a playground "pay" with their time and labor.

Physical constraints are another barrier. For example, while public highways are open to all, too many vehicles on the road create a traffic jam. Likewise, heavy demand on a public Wi-Fi network slows service for everyone. And, while water cycles throughout the planet—my clouds on Monday will be your rain on Tuesday—this vital resource is stretched among agriculture, manufacturing, and the needs of a growing population. Resources such as highways, the Internet, and water are thus vulnerable to congestion or overuse. Economists refer to them as *rival* given that providing access to an additional user can degrade the overall quality and diminish benefits to others (Daly & Farley, 2004). In contrast, nonrival resources, such as sunlight, can provide light to an unlimited number of people at once. (The sun does not dim each time someone is born.) Air or a beautiful vista have similar qualities; we can all breathe at once, and my enjoyment of a view doesn't lessen yours (assuming I'm not blocking you).

Ah, if only everything we needed was nonrival. But it's not. And this raises the uncomfortable question: If so much of what we need is rival, is it even possible to provide everyone with access?

This perennial dilemma is known as the "Tragedy of the Commons," the title of a classic article by biologist Garrett Hardin (1968). Hardin laid out the fundamental reality about "common-pool resources" (National Research Council, 2002): When access is fully open, increasing benefits to an individual can reduce them for everyone else, even if the resource is renewable (i.e., able to reproduce).

Hardin (1968) offered the example of herdsmen [sic] sharing a common pasture. Suppose there are 20 herders each grazing 10 cows, and Herder A decides to add an 11th head. Herder A fully reaps the gain, but the impacts (less forage, increased waste) are spread among all 20 herders. But because the immediate benefits outweigh the costs, each herder has a powerful incentive to "increase his herd without limit—in a world that is limited" (p. 1244). If all herdsmen follow suit, the influx of cows will degrade the pasture for everyone.

Hardin suggested that the shared nature of the Commons "remorselessly generates tragedy" (p. 1245). In this free-for-all predicament where self-interest seemingly trumps all, one response is to enclose and privatize the pasture. While that may curtail overgrazing, privatization doesn't guarantee the field will be divided fairly. If it's not, and instead goes to the highest bidder, what will become of the other herders?

At first glance, the most direct educational parallel to Hardin's congested pasture is the overcrowded classroom. While this is certainly a problem, there's a more fundamental tragedy: lack of access to quality learning opportunities. Unlike pastures or classroom spaces, which are rival, learning itself is limitless and nonrival; I can learn as much as I want without limiting your ability to do so. We can all devour an infinite amount of knowledge, and the benefits I gain should not undermine yours. And while educating each child has costs, equity demands that we provide quality education for all. That is true, unless I find a way to exclude you and make education a rivalry—in other words, turn the Commons into a commodity. This is exactly what's happening, as we'll explore in Part II. Students in poverty and students of color are excluded from the "pasture" of opportunity in ways that go far beyond class size or funding, which itself is inequitable (NCES, 2016a).

Exclusion and enclosure are phenomena both in and out of classrooms. And whether we are talking about the environment or learning, to avoid Hardin's tragedy, we must create ways to simultaneously sustain the Commons while providing equitable access. The role of government, communities, private markets, or individual effort is a debate we'll come to later. But regardless of the means, we must value each individual enough to at least give them a fair shot. A person's chances of thriving, surviving, or even dying should not be determined by who they are or where they live. Yet, we face a world in which entire populations are excluded from the ability to meet even basic needs.

Our goals of sustainability and social justice thus hinge on two conditions: interdependence and equity—whether we recognize the former and commit to the latter. But this hinges on something even deeper: the stories we tell about human nature. Do we believe that people are innately self-interested, motivated only by the prospect of that extra cow and quick to slam the gate on others? Or do we believe we are born with the capacity for empathy and cooperating for the common good?

The Story We Want comes down to this: It must (a) support well-being for all, (b) sustain ecological and cultural systems, and (c) provide equitable access.

What's at stake? Everything. Where are we headed? That remains to be seen in Chapters 2 and 3.

Questions

1. What are the benefits and challenges of seeing the world in a more connected way?
2. What are the implications for you as an educator?
3. What additional questions does this raise?

Notes

1 Food sovereignty broadens the concept of food security by factoring in cultural appropriateness, environmental sustainability, and self-determination in defining agricultural systems.
2 "Low income" means that a student is eligible for free lunch or reduced lunch, measured in terms of the poverty threshold of $24,257 for a household of four. Students from households with incomes at or below 130% of the poverty level qualify for free lunch; students from households with incomes between 130% and 185% of the poverty level qualify for reduced-price meals.

References

Atkinson, S., & Davey, M. (2017, June 14). 5 charged with involuntary manslaughter in Flint water crisis. *The New York Times*. Retrieved from https://www.nytimes.com/2017/06/14/us/flint-water-crisis-manslaughter.html

Ben-Shahar, T. (2007). *Happier: Learn the secrets to daily joy and lasting fulfillment*. New York, NY: McGraw-Hill Education.

Bombay, A., Matheson, K., & Anisman, H. (2009). Intergenerational trauma: Convergence of multiple processes among first nations peoples in Canada. *Journal de la Santé Autochtone, 5*(3), 6–47.

Bombay, A., Matheson, K., & Anisman, H. (2014). The intergenerational effects of Indian Residential Schools: Implications for the concept of historical trauma. *Transcultural Psychiatry, 51*(3), 320–338.

Brown, E. (2015, August 24). Map: How student poverty has increased since the Great Recession. *The Washington Post.* Retrieved from https://www.washingtonpost.com/news/education/wp/2015/08/24/map-how-student-poverty-has-increased-since-the-great-recession

Brown, V. A., Harris, J. A., & Russell, J. Y. (Eds.). (2010). *Tackling wicked problems through the transdisciplinary imagination.* London, UK: Earthscan.

Bullard, R. D. (Ed.). (2005). *The quest for environmental justice: Human rights and the politics of pollution.* San Francisco, CA: Sierra Club Books.

Centers for Disease Control and Prevention. (2016). About the CDC–Kaiser ACE study. Retrieved from https://www.cdc.gov/violenceprevention/acestudy/about.html

Clayton, S., Manning, C. M., Krygsman, K., & Speiser, M. (2017). *Mental health and our changing climate: Impacts, implications, and guidance.* Washington, DC: American Psychological Association and ecoAmerica.

Coleman, J. S., Campbell, E. Q., Hobson, C. J., McPartland, J., Mood, A. M., Weinfeld, F. D., & York, R. L. (1965). *Equality of educational opportunity.* Washington, DC: U.S. Department of Education, National Center for Educational Statistics.

Daly, H., & Farley, J. (2004). *Ecological economics: Principles and applications.* Washington, DC: Island Press.

Earth Charter Initiative. (2016). *Earth charter around the world.* Retrieved from http://earthcharter.org

Fischbach, S. (2005). Schools on toxic sites: An environmental injustice for school children. *Human Rights, 32*(2). Retrieved from https://www.americanbar.org/publications/human_rights_magazine_home/human_rights_vol32_2005/fall2005/hr_Fall05_toxicsites.html

Food and Agricultural Organization of the United Nations. (2012). *Livestock and landscapes.* Retrieved from http://www.fao.org/docrep/018/ar591e/ar591e.pdf

Food and Agricultural Organization of the United Nations, International Fund for Agricultural Development, & World Food Programme. (2015). *The state of food insecurity in the world 2015. Meeting the 2015 international hunger targets: Taking stock of uneven progress.* Rome, Italy: FAO.

Hansen, J., Kharecha, P., Sato, M., Masson-Delmotte, V., Ackerman, F., Beerling, D. J., … Zachos, J. C. (2013). Assessing "dangerous climate change": Required reduction of carbon emissions to protect young people, future generations and nature. *PLOS ONE, 8*(12). doi:10.1371/journal.pone.0081648

Hardin, G. (1968). The tragedy of the commons. *Science, 162*(3859), 1243–1248.

Hawken, P. (2007). *Blessed unrest: How the largest movement in the world came into being and why no one saw it coming.* New York, NY: Viking Penguin.

Hoegh-Guldberg, O., Mumby, P. J., Hooten, A. J., Steneck, R. S., Greenfield, P., Gomez, E., … Hatziolos, M. E. (2007). Coral reefs under rapid climate change and ocean acidification. *Science, 318*(5857), 1737–1742.

Hornborg, A., McNeill, J. R., & Martinez-Alier, J. (Eds.). (2007). *Rethinking environmental history: World-system history and global environmental change.* Lanham, MD: AltaMira Press.

Kasperson, R. E., & Kasperson, J. X. (2001). *Climate change, vulnerability and social justice.* Stockholm, Sweden: Stockholm Environment Institute.

Kena, G., Musu-Gillette, L., Robinson, J., Wang, X., Rathbun, A., Zhang, J., ... Dunlop Velez, E. (2015). *The condition of education 2015* (NCES 2015–144). Washington, DC: U.S. Department of Education, National Center for Educational Statistics.

Kurth, J. (2016, March 31). Detroit hits residents on water shut-offs as businesses slide. *The Detroit News.* Retrieved from http://www.detroitnews.com/story/news/local/detroit-city/2016/03/31/detroit-water-shutoffs/82497496

Martusewicz, R. A., Edmundson, J., & Lupinacci, J. (2011). *Ecojustice education: Toward diverse, democratic, and sustainable communities.* Abingdon, UK: Routledge.

Maxwell, L. A. (2014, August 19). U.S. school enrollment hits majority–minority milestone. *Education Week.* Retrieved from http://www.edweek.org/ew/articles/2014/08/20/01demographics.h34.html

McGowan, P. O., & Szyf, M. (2010). The epigenetics of social adversity in early life: Implications for mental health outcomes. *Neurobiology of Disease, 39*(1), 66–72.

Meadows, D. H. (2008). *Thinking in systems: A primer.* White River Junction, VT: Chelsea Green.

Melamed, C., & Samman, E. (2013). *Equity, inequality and human development in a post-2015 framework.* New York, NY: United Nations Development Programme.

National Academy of Sciences. (2014). *Climate change: Evidence and causes.* Washington, DC: The National Academies Press. Retrieved from https://www.nap.edu/catalog/18730/climate-change-evidence-and-causes

National Assessment of Educational Progress. (2018). *2017 NAEP mathematics & reading assessments.* Retrieved from https://www.nationsreportcard.gov/reading_math_2017_highlights

National Center for Education Statistics. (2014). *Percentage distribution of highest level of educational attainment of spring 2002 high school sophomores in 2012, by socioeconomic status (SES).* Retrieved from https://nces.ed.gov/programs/coe/indicator_tva.asp

National Center for Education Statistics. (2015a). *Graduation rate from first institution attended for first-time, full-time bachelor's degree-seeking students at 4-year postsecondary institutions, by race/ethnicity, time to completion, sex, control of institution, and acceptance rate: Selected cohort entry years, 1996 through 2008.* Retrieved from https://nces.ed.gov/programs/digest/d15/tables/dt15_326.10.asp

National Center for Education Statistics. (2015b). *Percentage of 18- to 24-year-olds enrolled in degree-granting postsecondary institutions, by level of institution and sex and race/ethnicity of student: 1970 through 2014.* Retrieved from https://nces.ed.gov/programs/digest/d15/tables/dt15_302.60.asp

National Center for Education Statistics. (2015c). *Percentage of recent high school completers enrolled in 2-year and 4-year colleges, by income level: 1975 through 2014.* Retrieved from https://nces.ed.gov/programs/digest/d15/tables/dt15_302.30.asp

National Center for Education Statistics. (2016a). *The condition of education 2016 at a glance.* Retrieved from https://nces.ed.gov/pubs2016/2016144_ataglance.pdf

National Center for Education Statistics. (2016b). *Average National Assessment of Educational Progress (NAEP) mathematics scale score, by sex, race/ethnicity, and grade: Selected years, 1990 through 2015.* Retrieved from https://nces.ed.gov/programs/digest/d15/tables/dt15_222.10.asp

National Center for Education Statistics. (2016c). *Average National Assessment of Educational Progress (NAEP) reading scale score, by sex, race/ethnicity, and grade: Selected years, 1992 through 2015.* Retrieved from https://nces.ed.gov/programs/digest/d15/tables/dt15_221.10.asp

National Center for Education Statistics. (2016d). *Percentage of high school dropouts among persons 16 to 24 years old (status dropout rate), by income level, and percentage distribution of status dropouts, by labor force status and years of school completed: 1970 through 2015*. Retrieved from https://nces.ed.gov/programs/digest/d16/tables/dt16_219.75.asp

National Center for Education Statistics. (2016e). *Status dropout rates of 16- to 24-year-olds, by race/ethnicity and nativity: 2015*. Retrieved from https://nces.ed.gov/programs/coe/indicator_coj.asp

National Research Council. (2002). *The drama of the commons*. Washington, DC: The National Academies Press.

Newman, P., Beatley, T., & Boyer, H. (2009). *Resilient cities: Responding to peak oil and climate change*. Washington, DC: Island Press.

Nolet, V. (2015). *Educating for sustainability: Principles and practices for teachers*. New York, NY: Routledge.

Non-Communicable Diseases Risk Factor Collaboration. (2016). Trends in adult body-mass index in 200 countries from 1975 to 2014: A pooled analysis of 1698 population-based measurement studies with 19.2 million participants. *The Lancet, 387*(10026), 1377–1396.

Nunavut Climate Change Centre. (n.d.). *Climate change impacts*. Retrieved from http://www.climatechangenunavut.ca/en/understanding-climate-change/climate-change-impact

Ogden, C. L., Carroll, M. D., Fryar, C. D., & Flegal, K. M. (2015, November). Prevalence of obesity among adults and youth: United States, 2011–2014. *NCHS Data Brief* (No. 219). Retrieved from https://www.ncbi.nlm.nih.gov/pubmed/26633046

Organisation for Economic Co-operation and Development. (2017). *Income inequality*. Retrieved from https://data.oecd.org/inequality/income-inequality.htm

Reardon, S. (2011). The widening academic achievement gap between the rich and the poor: New evidence and possible explanations. In R. Murnane & G. Duncan (Eds.), *Whither opportunity? Rising inequality, schools, and children's life chances* (pp. 91–116). New York, NY: Russell Sage Foundation Press.

Reardon, S. F., & Owens, A. (2014). 60 years after Brown: Trends and consequences of school segregation. *Annual Review of Sociology, 40*(1), 199–218.

Renewable Energy Policy Network for the 21st Century. (2016). *Renewables 2016: Global status report*. Retrieved from http://www.ren21.net/wp-content/uploads/2016/10/REN21_GSR2016_FullReport_en_11.pdf

Rowe, J. (2013). *Our common wealth: The hidden economy that makes everything else work*. San Francisco, CA: Berrett-Koehler.

Shonkoff, J. P., Boyce, W. T., & McEwen, B. S. (2009). Neuroscience, molecular biology, and the childhood roots of health disparities: Building a new framework for health promotion and disease prevention. *JAMA, 301*(21), 2252–2259.

Shonkoff, J. P., Garner, A. S., Siegel, B. S., Dobbins, M. I., Earls, M. F., McGuinn, L., ... Wood, D. L. (2012). The lifelong effects of early childhood adversity and toxic stress. *Pediatrics, 129*(1), 232–246.

Sobel, D. (1996). *Beyond ecophobia: Reclaiming the heart in nature education*. Great Barrington, MA: Orion Society.

Spring, J. (2016). *Deculturalization and the struggle for equality: A brief history of the education of dominated cultures in the United States* (8th ed.). New York, NY: Routledge.

Stone, B., Hess, J. J., & Frumkin, H. (2010). Urban form and extreme heat events: Are sprawling cities more vulnerable to climate change than compact cities? *Environmental Health Perspectives, 118*(10), 1425–1428.

United Nations. (2016). *Sustainable development goals: 17 goals to transform our world.* Retrieved from http://www.un.org/sustainabledevelopment/sustainable-development-goals

United Nations Development Programme. (2011). *Human development report 2011. Sustainability and equity: A better future for all.* New York, NY: UNDP.

United Nations Economic and Social Council. (2016). *Progress towards the sustainable development goals: Report of the Secretary-General.* Retrieved from www.un.org/ga/search/view_doc.asp?symbol=E/2016/75&Lang=E

United Nations News Centre. (2016, May 3). Flint Michigan crisis "not just about water," UN rights experts say ahead of President Obama's visit. *UN News.* Retrieved from http://www.un.org/apps/news/story.asp?NewsID=53839#.WQct7cYpDIV

U.S. Department of Agriculture. (2017). Farmers' market SNAP support grants. Retrieved from https://www.fns.usda.gov/snap/farmers-market-snap-support-grants

U.S. Department of Agriculture Economic Research Service. (2017). Food access research atlas. Retrieved from https://www.ers.usda.gov/data-products/food-access-research-atlas

U.S. Department of Defense. (2015). *National security implications of climate-related risks and a changing climate.* Retrieved from http://archive.defense.gov/pubs/150724-congressional-report-on-national-implications-of-climate-change.pdf?source=govdelivery

U.S. Energy Information Administration. (2016). *International energy outlook 2016.* Retrieved from https://www.eia.gov/outlooks/archive/ieo16

U.S. Environmental Protection Agency. (n.d.). *Environmental justice.* Retrieved from https://www.epa.gov/environmentaljustice

2

THE DOMINANT NARRATIVE

The Story of More

Once upon a time ...

That's the age-old beginning to countless fairy tales and fables. The phrase signals fiction, and that's why it's an appropriate way to kick off this chapter, the Story of More, a tale rife with beliefs about ... well, you'll just have to keep reading. We'll frame the story using these questions:

- Who are the characters and what are their goals?
- How do the characters know whether they're on the right track?
- How did the story get started?
- How did this story get accepted as truth?
- Where is the story heading?

The answers to these questions will reveal the mindsets and values of our prevailing paradigm. Activities and discussions throughout will help you pinpoint whether or how they're embedded in your curriculum. You'll take these insights with you throughout the book, building the knowledge base needed to reframe units and courses in Part III. Let's get rolling.

Who Are the Characters and What Are Their Goals?

Every good story has a compelling lead, so let's begin by introducing ours: *homo economicus,* aka "economic man" (Gintis, 2000; Thaler, 2000).[1] Coined by economists in the late nineteenth century, *homo economicus* is a construct of human nature defined by self-interest and the pursuit of individual gain. Sounds sort of selfish, doesn't it? Not in this story. That's because the me-first motive is presumed to be an innate human trait—one that overrides others such as empathy or cooperativeness (Baumgärtner, Becker, Faber, & Manstetten, 2006; Bowles & Gintis, 1993).

The Story of More is all about *individualism*, a conception of self removed from community. *Individuality*, the uniqueness of each person, is an expendable distraction. And interdependence? That's an inconvenience that entangles our character in pesky social and ecological relationships.

The goal of maximizing self-benefit drives the primary mode of interaction: zero-sum competition, a game in which one winner reigns over multiple losers (Mykleby & Porter, 2011). Because only one can win, "Others" loom as adversaries and threats. We have no choice but to subjugate them. Hierarchy is necessary and equality is impossible. The victors safeguard their dominance through ranking and sorting, legitimized by an unquestioned belief in their superiority. In this storyline, only the most capable deserve rewards, and that means winners are inherently (dare we say genetically?) better. Conversely, losers fail due to defective character or a deprived culture. It's all about meritocracy, and market-based competition ensures "everyone gets what they deserve" (Monbiot, 2016).

Because *homo economicus* is our main character, it seems only fitting to provide a name. With a nod to the chapter title, we'll use the eponymous Moore. (You can put your own image to it.) Moore is not presented as a caricature of capitalism. Rather, Moore is an archetype—a representation of social actors bound by a system that requires putting self above others. Behaviors that seem self-serving or even harmful to others are actually logical responses to the story's rules. As the chapter unfolds, we'll scrutinize the incentives that motivate Moore and Friends as well as the rationalizations behind their actions.

How Do the Characters Know Whether They're on the Right Track?

Moore's motivations launch him on a quest to get ahead, defined in this story by more: more profits, more resources, more market share—in other words, economic growth measured in quantitative terms. To assess his progress, he looks to short-term measures of daily profits, quarterly returns, or annual growth in the gross domestic product (GDP). The GDP carries particular significance for Moore, so let's take a closer look.

The GDP is the sum value of economic activity and is defined as "the total market value of the output of goods and services produced by labor and property located in the United States" (Bureau of Economic Analysis, 2015). The GDP includes government spending, consumer spending (typically two-thirds of the total), investments, and the difference between exports and imports. A related indicator, the gross national product (GNP) includes only goods and services produced within a country's geographic boundaries.

Moore and Friends constantly track the GDP because they believe that when the GDP is up, life is indisputably better (Cobb, Halstead, & Rowe, 1995). It's a "more = better" worldview that, by some measures, makes sense. After acquiring basic needs, Moore might spend money on recreation or other experiences that can enhance life. And for people who don't have adequate food or shelter, *more* of these necessities are definitely an improvement. Sounds logical. But is the assertion that "growth = benefits" an ironclad truth? To find out, let's get to the bottom of the GDP's own story.

With quantitative growth the goal, the GDP measures all monetary transactions—regardless of their impacts on the environment or society. A detrimental activity such as crime is counted as *positive* because it adds to the bottom line in the form of costly lawsuits and other spending. For example, the United Kingdom's Office for National Statistics reported that illegal drugs and sex work added £12.3 billion to their GDP in 2014 (Linning, 2014). Conversely, nonmonetized transactions, however beneficial, do nothing for the GDP. Because no money changes hands when you volunteer, walk to work, or grow your own tomatoes, the contributions to health and community do not register in the GDP's ledgers. But why should Moore care? If it can't be bought or sold, it isn't important, right? From an educational perspective, we see the parallels in the primacy of test scores as the measure of success rather than a holistic appraisal of children's well-being. (We'll dive into this in Part II.)

The GDP has another fatal flaw: It fails to account for the life-sustaining benefits provided by the environment, such the production of oxygen by trees. These *ecosystem services* are the gifts of the ecological Commons. But in a story where money defines value, a tree is deemed worthless and *unproductive* until it is harvested or contributes to property values. In the Story of More, the environment is only a set of commodities—a trough of *natural resources* at Moore's disposal (Baumgärtner et al., 2006).

True, the GDP was never intended to serve as an integrated measure of success. Simon Kuznets, the Nobel Prize-winning architect of the GDP, alerted policymakers to its limitations in the early 1930s. "The welfare of a nation can scarcely be inferred from a measurement of national income," he wrote in a 1934 report to Congress (p. 7). "Goals for 'more' growth should specify of what and for what" (as cited in Desha, Hargroves, & Smith, 2010, p. 47). Likewise, in a 1968 speech, Robert Kennedy pointed out that the GNP counts "air pollution and cigarette advertising ... the loss of our natural wonder ... [and] nuclear warheads" while ignoring "the health of our children, the quality of their education or the joy of their play" (para. 22). He added "[The GNP] measures neither our wit nor our courage, neither our wisdom nor our learning. ... It measures everything in short, except that which makes life worthwhile."

These cautions, however, have gone unheeded. The GDP has acquired totemic stature, with Moore and Friends monitoring the metric as if it were the pulse of the nation (Cobb et al., 1995). If the GDP is rising, times must be getting better. If it's down, policymakers struggle to restore growth and the well-being assumed to go with it. And, while a rising GDP might signal new jobs or other positive changes, as a singular yardstick, its limitations are clear.

Nonetheless, some of Moore's colleagues get so exuberant about growth that they dismiss inescapable ecological constraints, such as the finite nature of nonrenewable resources. Instead, these soothsayers spin the magical tale that human ingenuity, technology, and the free market will always find a substitute or work-around. Running out of oil? C'mon—isn't that what they said the last time we discovered a new deposit? Overloading the atmosphere with carbon? Technology—perhaps a carbon vacuum?—will make short work of that. Think deforestation is a problem? *Wrong.* Deforestation in medieval Europe led to a new fuel—coal (Nef, 1977). Blessing in disguise! (Never mind that fossil fuels—the alleged silver lining—only exacerbate the need for forests, our natural carbon vacuum.)

The guru of this school of thought is Julian Simon (1996), who laid out the giddy premise on the cover of *The Ultimate Resource*: "Natural resources ... food supply ... pressures of population growth ... Every trend in material human welfare is improving, and promises to continue to do so—indefinitely" (*ellipses in original*). Chapter titles include "Should We Conserve Resources for Others' Sake?," "Coercive Recycling, Forced Conservation, and Free-Market Alternatives," and "When Will We Run Out of Oil? Never!"

Economist Herman Daly, former head of the World Bank, calls Simon's work "a coarse mixture of simple fallacy, omission of contrary evidence from his own expert sources and gross statistical misinterpretation" (Daly, 1982, p. 39). Simon's heir apparent, Bjørn Lomborg (2001), carried the thinking forward in *The Skeptical Environmentalist*, a book that ignited a firestorm of criticism and debate (Whelan, 2002). And while a complete analysis of the sleight-of-hand reasoning is beyond the scope of this chapter, the storyline is clear: Unlimited growth of material output is both desirable and possible.

Activity 2.1: More, Better, or Both?

Consider the statement from Simon Kuznets, architect of the GDP: "Goals for 'more' growth should specify of what and for what" (as cited in Desha et al., 2010, p. 47). In your view, what should be growing? How can we determine when more is better? Let's explore this in the following activity.

Directions:

1. Below are several examples of hypothetical changes in a community. Read each and decide whether the change brought about economic growth (i.e., more money), whether the change made the community better, or whether the change accomplished both.
2. Write the letter of the example in the correct part of the Venn diagram (see Figure 2.1). If you're not sure where to place an example, identify the information you'd need to decide.
3. (a) Your neighborhood garden has a bumper crop and free vegetables are distributed to local families.
   (b) A local bike-to-work campaign is effective, resulting in fewer cars on the road.

Growth (More Money)   A Better Community

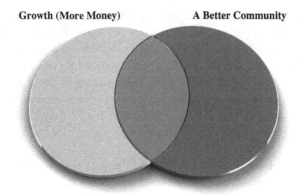

FIGURE 2.1 More, Better, or Both?

(c) The community health clinic receives a large donation and uses the money to hire medical staff and provide care to children who would not otherwise get it.

(d) A company with no ties to the region builds a luxury condominium development on a former farm.

(e) Your community opens a casino to increase tax revenue.

(f) To focus on reading, an elementary school cuts art and music, and reduces time for science and social studies. Standardized test scores go up.

(g) A district revamps its *key indicators,* traditionally based on test scores, to include teacher satisfaction, student health, and community and parental involvement.

Discussion Questions

1. What conclusions can you draw about the relationship between money and well-being?
2. Where would Moore place each example in the diagram?
3. Are there examples with inherent tensions that make categorization difficult?
4. If growth in the GDP is the measure of success, what is the measure of success in education? What is the official goal?
5. What are the indicators of success for this goal? How do we measure it?

How Did the Story Get Started?

A complex tale like the Story of More develops over many years—in this case, centuries—with roots in Western philosophy, science, and economics. By *Western,* we mean the systems and societies associated with Europe, as influenced by

Ancient Greek and Roman civilization and Judeo-Christian religions (Birken, 1992). What follows is not a condemnation of the West's prominent thinkers, nor of the inventions, arts, literature, and ideas they gave the world. Moreover, we are not suggesting that oppression and injustice are problems unique to the West, or even its sole outcome. Instead, our intent is to understand how the Story of More came to dominate and the belief systems that drove it all.

Religious Influences

Many indigenous and pagan (pre-Judeo-Christian) religions connect nature with spirituality (Hughes, 1975). Eastern belief systems, such as Buddhism and Shintoism, emphasize humans' connections to the natural world (Devall & Sessions, 1985).

Teachings about the environment are found in the Bible, but translations and interpretations vary. Consider the account of creation, Genesis 1:28. The King James Bible says that humans should "replenish the earth, and subdue it: and have dominion ... over every living thing that moveth upon the earth." The New American Bible uses the phrase "rule over," while the International Standard version states that God commanded humans to "be masters" over nature. To some scholars, these translations legitimize an anthropocentric domination over nature (Hiebert, 1996; White, 1967). However, others interpret this as a mandate for stewardship, not domination (Duitsman, 1987; Ehrenfeld & Bentley, 1985). Either way, common associations of human and nonhuman animals (e.g., "What a pig!") denigrate other animals and situate people apart from them (Goatly, 2006). This does not mean that Judeo-Christian faiths are inherently antienvironmental. On the contrary, these and other religions are drawing upon their respective theologies to advance ecological stewardship within and across faiths (The Interfaith Center for Sustainable Development, 2017). We'll explore this more in Chapter 3.

Economic and Scientific Influences

Around 12,000 years ago across multiple continents, the agricultural revolution set into motion profound changes in human social structures. Archaeologists believe that up until that time, people lived as hunters and gatherers in relatively egalitarian bands given that mobility prevented the accumulation of food and other resources that can create power imbalances (Woodburn, 1982). In this world, Moore had yet to be conceived.

But agriculture transformed society by producing the food surpluses that enabled the development of permanent settlements. Freed from the constant need to hunt and forage, people began to specialize in other types of work, such as pottery or clothing production. Stocks of food also created the need for bureaucrats, rulers, and organized military structures to protect and manage resources and growing populations (Barker, 2009). As distinct professions and roles emerged, so did class stratifications (Smith, 1998). Just like the seeds of wheat and barley, the seeds of Moore took root.

Fast-forward to the era of colonialism[2] (1400s–1800s), a period when imperialist ideologies reshaped the world (Said, 1998). During these centuries, colonizing countries such as England, Spain, and France occupied North and South America, Africa, and Asia, exploiting indigenous populations, extracting resources, and installing rulers (often cultivating a class of native elites; McMichael, 2012; Moore Lappé, 1971). As a precursor to modern globalization, colonialism turned the ecological Commons into a commodity, elevating the importance of markets. Economic and social structures placed people over people, culture over culture, and people over the environment. This era intensified the role of domination as both a means and an ends to the Story of More. Our friend Moore was starting to grow up.

The era of colonialism overlapped with The Enlightenment (1640–1850), a transformative time in Western philosophy, science, and economics. The Enlightenment strengthened the domination narrative through a new idea: Humans can control nature if we see it as a machine. The English philosopher Sir Francis Bacon (1561–1626) was a thought leader of the day. His publication *Novum Organum* (1620/2000) outlined a new system of reductionism: breaking down natural forces to their individual parts in order to master and subjugate them. He wrote, "By art and the hand" nature can be "forced out of her natural state and squeezed and molded" (cited in Merchant, 2001, p. 279). Invoking a God-given right to dominate, Bacon (1620/2000) added that by "extend[ing] the power and dominion of the human race itself over the universe," humans could "recover the right over nature which belongs to it by divine bequest" (p. 280). In 1637, René Descartes (1596–1650) advanced this way of thinking in *Discourse on Method and Meditations on First Philosophy* (1637/2005). He asserted that "knowing the force and the action" can render humans the "masters and possessors of nature" (p. 28). Extending the thinking to property rights, John Locke (1632–1704) asserted that altering the land confers ownership. In *Two Treatises of Government* (1689), he wrote, "As much land as a man tills, plants, improves, cultivates, and can use the product of, so much is his property" (p. 213). Control toil to stake your claim: How could Moore disagree with logic like that?

The Industrial Revolution

Enlightenment thinkers gave Moore new vocabulary to express the concept of *power over,* that is, domination. This set the stage for the next big plot development: the Industrial Revolution (roughly 1760–1840). Before then, the scale of economic activity was largely limited by the availability of energy, whether provided by people (often enslaved), nonhuman animals, or the mechanical power from windmills or water wheels (McKibben, 2007). This changed with the introduction of technologies that harnessed coal as a primary fuel. In 1712, Thomas Newcomen, a British inventor, developed a coal-powered steam engine, and in the 1760s, James Watts, a Scottish technician, improved its efficiency. This unleashed the energy needed to mass produce iron and textiles, two important economic sectors of this period (Rolt & Allen, 1977). You can imagine how excited Moore was—at last, a way to accelerate growth!

The budding industrial economy in England got a helping hand from the privatization of commonly held rural land—the very type of resource that Hardin warned is doomed to be degraded. With the principles of property rights well-established, England's parliament passed a series of Enclosure Acts that converted large swaths of cropland to private pasture in order to increase wool production (Cameron, 1985). Many of the acts took place between 1750 and 1830, displacing rural populations that migrated to swelling cities to join the industrial labor pool (Wood, 2002).

Colonialism, the Enlightenment, and the Industrial Revolution were thus formative centuries that shaped Moore's worldview. Sitting at the knee of the day's prominent thinkers, our character absorbed the Story of More and accepted the premise that this is how things should be: growth as the goal, competition the means, Us over Them, and people over nature. It's a story that yields undeniable economic benefits to those in power. But do they also pay a price? (Stay tuned.)

Discussion Questions

1. Which historical developments do you think have had the greatest influence over the development of the narrative and Moore's acceptance of it? Why?
2. What are other pivotal historical points in this story?
3. Thinking over your own education, what messages did you get about humans' relationship with the environment? Consider teachings from schools, religion, family, and media.
4. What messages are in your current curriculum or discipline about human-environmental relationships or anthropocentrism? Examples: A first-grade book on animals does not mention humans. Lessons about the rainforest do not include learning about the people who have long lived there.
5. Can you find examples of reductionist thinking in your curriculum? For example, Next Generation Engineering Standard HS-ETS1-3 states, "Design a solution to a complex real-world problem by breaking it down into smaller, more manageable problems that can be solved through engineering." When can engineering solutions be helpful? When might it be better to prevent the problem in the first place? How would such a standard read?

6. For social science, science, and language arts educators: Identify three historical, economic, or social topics or eras that are addressed in your curriculum (e.g., ancient empires, globalization). How does your unit or course present social hierarchies? Are they acknowledged, directly or indirectly? What are the underlying assumptions about the relationships among cultures and nations?

How Did This Story Become Accepted as Truth?

By the mid-nineteenth century, accelerating economic and social change had delineated power disparities among people, cultures, races, and nations—with Moore on top. Oppression based on race, class, and gender, while having existed in many forms throughout history, was now institutionalized at a global scale. In industrialized countries such as the United States and England, urban areas grew rapidly, but often without the necessary infrastructure and sanitation. Crowded tenements, open sewage, and diseases such as cholera proliferated. These conditions, along with low wages and brutal working conditions, sharpened class divisions.

The spread of social problems required a response, and that posed a prickly problem for Moore: Truly addressing the underlying forces could topple the whole system. Can't have that. No, poverty and disease needed another explanation—and it had better be a good one. The solution? Distract from structural causes by blaming the problems on individuals. In this alternative account, the villain was not unjust *systems* but rather unfit *people*. The theory seemed solid since it was couched in an aura of scholarship. Thomas Malthus (1766–1834), a British professor, helped lay the foundation with his 1789 publication, *Essay on the Principle of Population*. In this infamous work, Malthus warned that exponential population growth would outstrip food supply, resulting in widespread famine and misery. Logically, society should adopt policies that curb population growth through the *natural* attrition of the poor—the lazy, unemployed underclass who did not deserve to survive. Appealing to religion, Malthus (1803) stated, "The laws of nature, which are the laws of God" do not guarantee "cover" (p. 425, quoted in Gaston, 2016, p. 199). For Malthus (and Moore), hunger and disease served as a divine social improvement plan. Conversely, interventions such as public aid, education, or health care were immoral because they simply enabled the undeserving to reproduce (Chase, 1980).

Malthus's work came to the attention of Charles Darwin (1809–1882), whose research on population dynamics and variations among organisms led to the theory of natural selection presented in *On the Origin of Species* (1859). The basic theory is that the organisms with the most favorable variations for survival are more likely to reproduce. For example, a yellow moth that stands out on a tree trunk is more likely to be eaten by a predator than is a brown moth, which blends in. By surviving, the brown moth reproduces and passes on its favorable variation to the next generation.

Human variations did not escape Darwin's interest. In *The Descent of Man* (1888), he wrote about the "races of man," viewing them "in the same spirit as a naturalist would any other animal" (p. 167). But his interests went beyond pure observation; in the book, he considered "arguments in favor of and opposed to ranking the so-called races" and "the value of the differences between them under a classificatory point of view" (p. 166). In *The Voyage of the Beagle* (1909), Darwin simultaneously derided the "savage Fuegian" of South America (p. 235), praised the "constitutional gaiety of the negro" (p. 520), and marveled at just how similar the "lower" races are to Whites once "they" are "improved" (p. 234). Rather than seeing inequality as fixed, Darwin took the paternalistic view that although others are inferior, they are salvageable through Westernization (Gould, 1996). Interestingly, Darwin was also a fervent abolitionist who opposed the use of then-accepted biological hierarchies as a rationale for slavery (Gould, 1993).

Nonetheless, Moore and Friends co-opted Darwin's ideas to justify socially constructed class stratification, a pseudoscience known as "Social Darwinism." Leading the pack was Herbert Spencer (1820–1903), a British philosopher and sociologist (Leonard, 2009). (It was actually Spencer, not Darwin, who coined the term "survival of the fittest.") Like Malthus, Spencer opposed policies and programs to improve sanitation, health care, or working conditions. Survival of the fittest also became a rallying cry of nineteenth-century tycoons (including John D. Rockefeller, Sr., who befriended Spencer) to explain the *evolution* of their corporate monopolies as a natural occurrence (Bergman, 2001). That all made sense to Moore and Friends; after all, if the profit motive is innate as they contended, capitalism is a marker of an advanced society. That makes bartering and sharing mere primitive ancestors of the market economy.

The burgeoning field of genetics continued to permeate social discourse into the early twentieth century. The cachet of science gave credence to social improvement policies designed to sort the fit from the unfit, which at the time included the "feebleminded," epileptics, paupers, and criminals (Cohen, 2016). One prominent policy example is eugenics, a form of "selective breeding" that encourages "superior" people to have children—and prevents reproduction among the inferior. Like Malthus and Spencer, eugenicists attributed social problems to individual flaws—in this case, defective genes. To check the problem at its source, champions of eugenics, including Sir Francis Galton (1822–1911) and Charles Davenport (1886–1944), advocated for forced sterilization (Challis, 2013), casting it as a noble endeavor in the interest of the common good. The movement gained traction in the United States and abroad, bolstered by the support of medical professionals, universities, charitable organizations, and clergy (although Catholics opposed it; Cruz & Berson, 2001). And while critics pointed to flawed science, state-level efforts to legalize eugenic sterilization accelerated, culminating in the 1927 Supreme Court case *Buck v. Bell,* which upheld the practice on the grounds that the benefits to society outweighed any harm to individuals.

Social Darwinism and eugenics assigns human worth based on a fabricated genetic hierarchy. While it's no longer acceptable to rank based on genetic inferiority (although some still try), it *is* acceptable—and all too common—to rank based on presumed cultural inferiority. As we'll see in Part II, bringing this thinking into education has grave consequences for students.

Whether in society or in classrooms, the domination ideology draws a sharp line between Us (the winners) and Them (the losers). They are the "Different Ones" who are "less competent, less skilled, less knowing—in short, less human" (Ryan, 1972, p. 10). Dehumanization cements the charade, enabling us to rest easy after we wash our hands of Others. And because They are not like Us, we're absolved from learning their story—let alone how it's entangled with ours.

Our purpose here is not to blame Moore as a selfish individual, but rather to understand that in this narrative, Moore's behaviors and rationalizations are both logical and necessary to win a zero-sum competition. Yet this exacts a psychological toll. To maintain the status quo, Moore and Friends must retreat from the Others and deny their common humanity and the equal value of all people. This "psychic self-preservation" (Ladson-Billings, 1998, p. 13) insulates the winners and legitimizes the subjugation their position depends upon. To prop up the flimsy ruse, those on top may supra-humanize themselves, proclaiming inborn superiority where none exists. It's a useful crutch under the weight of such a farce, but it can carry a heavy price: a distorted identity, corrosive social and emotional isolation, a reliance on stereotyping, and diminished empathy and compassion (Glick, 2005; Kraus, Côté, & Keltner, 2010; Stellar, Manzo, Kraus, & Keltner, 2012). Yet even unwitting participation in the scheme does not excuse Moore and Friends from the repercussions of their actions. Indeed, we must all wake up to the power dynamics that define social structures. It's a risky proposition, because once we become aware, we must decide how to respond.

So which is more difficult? Taking off the mask or leaving it on? Ending the game or staying in it? Could there be a way to change the game? In Part II, we'll apply the questions to education.

Where Is the Story Headed?

In the twentieth century, the Story of More evolved within the framework of international "development," accelerated by the establishment of global institutions such as the International Monetary Fund (IMF). The IMF was one outcome of the 1944 Bretton Woods conference, a gathering of more than 700 delegates from 44 Allied Nations focused on stabilizing the global financial system in the wake of World War II. Development began to take on a nobler role as the key to international poverty reduction. "Developed" thus became synonymous with "industrialized" as the path to well-being. In his 1949 inaugural address, President Harry Truman promoted the deployment of the nation's industrial might to "the improvement and growth of underdeveloped areas."

Fast-forward to the 1970s. Corporate profits were falling, in part due to rising wages and oil prices (Hursh, 2005). Businesses pointed a finger at governmental interventions, such as expanded workers' rights, and pushed for deregulation and limited government involvement. These are among the defining traits of neoliberalism (Gill, 2003; Monbiot, 2016). Like the Story of More, neoliberalism is grounded in competition and free markets that "recast inequality as virtuous" because it provides motivation to those at the bottom (Monbiot, 2016, para. 5). At the global level, neoliberalism has driven decades of globalization and the associated agreements and institutions such as the North American Free Trade Agreement (NAFTA) and the World Trade Organization (WTO; Thacker, 1999).

The discourse of economic hierarchy has seeped into our everyday language, with "First World/Developed" and "Third World/Undeveloped/Developing" as proxies for "rich/industrialized" and "poor." With claims of genetic superiority no longer accepted (by most), inequality is often attributed to primitive cultures and backward ways that only Western concepts of success can correct (McMichael, 2012).

Clearly, eliminating poverty is rightfully an international priority (Sustainable Development Goal 1) alongside related goals such as improving education and restoring the environment. And while economic growth has enriched many, the grossly uneven prosperity discredits growth as *the* panacea for poverty (Daly, 1982). Nonetheless, the Story of More clings to the dogged belief that quantity inevitably leads to quality. It sounds great, but the true costs and benefits of trade deals such as NAFTA are neither conclusive nor equitable (Burfisher, Robinson, & Thierfelder, 2001; Congressional Budget Office, 2003).

We must also remember that not all corporations are bad or ruthlessly neoliberal. Movements such as corporate social responsibility, social entrepreneurship, Fair Trade, and the "triple bottom line" (people, planet, and prosperity) are ways businesses are integrating environmental and social justice concerns. Many corporations also see the writing on the wall regarding climate change and resource depletion. For example, a host of business leaders—including the CEO of Exxon Mobil—slammed President Trump's 2017 decision to withdraw the United States from the Paris climate agreement (Murray, 2017).

Despite these undercurrents of change, the Story of More's themes of consumption and individualism continue their worldwide expansion. Technology, from virtual reality to biotechnology, is the new marker of progress—a narrative our educational system touts as necessary to prepare students to compete in the global economy.

Again, this chapter is not meant to dismiss Western history or culture, but rather an attempt to understand the roots of a narrative that rewards domination.

In doing so, we uncover its inherent contradictions: On one hand, the Story of More prizes industriousness and proclaims itself a meritocracy. On the other, the game's need for many losers requires built-in barriers that block personal initiative from paying off. How can we expect everyone to achieve in a system designed for only one winner? The narrative operates on other flawed premises: Humans are separate from the environment, hierarchy is inevitable, and the economy operates outside of ecological constraints. By (willfully?) clinging to these fallacies, Moore and Friends undercut their claim to truth and render the story a work of science fiction. In Chapter 5, we'll examine the educational parallels to these beliefs and dynamics.

The Story of More is a sweeping saga penned by those in power for whom the story rings true. And like it or not, we must admit that many of us—myself included—benefit as well. (I'm pretty sure my computer was not made from locally sourced metals by a nonprofit organization raising money to eliminate child labor.) We're all in the story and can even replicate it in hidden ways.

So what would an alternative narrative look like? A new possibility awaits in Chapter 3.

Activity 2.2: Chapter Review

The Story of More introduced us to interconnected social and economic dynamics. But what does this have to do with education? We'll answer this fully in Part II, but in the meantime, let's do some foreshadowing through the following activity.

Directions:

Review the center column of Table 2.1, which summarizes key ideas of the Story of More. In the right-hand column, generate parallel educational connections that come to mind. An example is provided.

TABLE 2.1 Summary of the Dominant Narrative

	The Story of More	*Educational parallels*
Goal	Growth	*Raise test scores* *Prepare students to compete*
Indicators	Increased profits and GDP	
Assumptions	Growth will eliminate inequality	
Labels and identifiers	Developed, First World, modern, forward thinking, progress Undeveloped, Third World, primitive, backward	

Discussion Questions

1. Who or what is the hero of the story? Who or what is the villain?
2. What do you think it would take to shift the plot?
3. If Moore were to assign the Story of More a genre, what would it be? (Nonfiction? Fantasy? Science Fiction? Memoir?) What genre is Moore least likely to choose? Why?

Notes

1 *Homo economicus* can be an individual or a corporation. Corporations have legal personhood, a status affirmed by the 1888 Supreme Court case *Pembina Consolidated Silver Mining Co. v. Pennsylvania* and upheld in subsequent cases since then.
2 Many textbooks refer to the era of colonialism as the Age of Discovery, a Eurocentric title that recasts conquest as "discovery," e.g., Columbus's "discovery" of America.

References

Bacon, F. (2000). *Novum organon* (L. Jardine & M. Silverthorne, Trans. & Eds.). Cambridge, UK: Cambridge University Press. (Original work published in 1620)

Barker, G. (2009). *The agricultural revolution in prehistory: Why did foragers become farmers?* New York, NY: Oxford University Press.

Baumgärtner, S., Becker, C., Faber, M., & Manstetten, R. (2006). Relative and absolute scarcity of nature. Assessing the roles of economics and ecology for biodiversity conservation. *Ecological Economics, 59*(4), 487–498.

Bergman, J. (2001). *Darwin's influence on ruthless laissez-fair capitalism.* Retrieved from Institute for Creation Research website: http://www.icr.org/article/darwins-influence-ruthless-laissez-faire-capitalis

Birken, L. (1992). What is western civilization? *The History Teacher, 25*(4), 451–461. doi:10.2307/494353

Bowles, S., & Gintis, H. (1993). The revenge of homo economicus: Contested exchange and the revival of political economy. *Journal of Economic Perspectives, 7*(1), 83–102.

Bureau of Economic Analysis. (2015). *Measuring the economy: A primer on GDP and the national income and product accounts.* Retrieved from http://www.bea.gov/national/pdf/nipa_primer.pdf

Burfisher, M. E., Robinson, S., & Thierfelder, K. (2001). The impact of NAFTA on the United States. *The Journal of Economic Perspectives, 15*(1), 125–144. Retrieved from http://www.jstor.org.ezproxy.emich.edu/stable/2696544

Cameron, R. (1985). A new view of European industrialization. *The Economic History Review, 38*(1), 1–23.

Challis, D. (2013). *The archaeology of race: The eugenic ideas of Francis Galton and Flinders Petrie.* London, UK: Bloomsbury Academic.

Chase, A. (1980). *The legacy of Malthus: The social costs of the new scientific racism.* New York, NY: Knopf.

Cobb, C., Halstead, T., & Rowe, J. (1995, October). If the GDP is up, why is America down? *Atlantic Monthly, 276,* 59–77.

Cohen, A. (2016). *Imbeciles: The Supreme Court, American eugenics, and the sterilization of Carrie Buck*. New York, NY: Penguin.

Congressional Budget Office. (2003, May 1). *The effects of NAFTA on U.S.–Mexican trade and GDP*. Retrieved from https://www.cbo.gov/publication/14461

Cruz, B. C., & Berson, M. J. (2001). The American melting pot? Miscegenation laws in the United States. *OAH Magazine of History, 15*(4), 80–84.

Daly, H. (1982, January). Review of *The ultimate resource* by J. Simon. *Bulletin of the Atomic Scientists*, 39–42.

Darwin, C. (1859). *On the origin of species*. London, UK: John Murray.

Darwin, C. (1888). *The descent of man and selection in relation to sex* (2nd ed.). London, UK: John Murray.

Darwin, C. (1909). *The voyage of the Beagle* (Vol. 29). New York, NY: P.F. Collier & Son.

Descartes, R. (2005). *Discourse on method and meditations on first philosophy* (E. Haldane, Trans.). Stilwell, KS: Digireads.com. (Original work published in 1637)

Desha, C., Hargroves, C., & Smith, M. H. (2010). *Cents and sustainability: Securing our common future by decoupling economic growth from environmental pressures*. New York, NY: Routledge.

Devall, B., & Sessions, G. (1985). *Deep ecology: Living as if nature mattered*. Layton, UT: Gibbs Smith.

Duitsman, M. A. (1987). *Ecology and theology: Christian responses to Lynn White Jr.* (Doctoral dissertation, California State University, Northridge). Retrieved from http://scholarworks.csun.edu/handle/10211.3/130567

Ehrenfeld, D., & Bentley, P. J. (1985). Judaism and the practice of stewardship. *Judaism, 34*(3), 301–311.

Gaston, L. (2016). Natural law and unnatural families in Martineau's *Illustrations of political economy*. *Nineteenth-Century Contexts, 38*(3), 195–207.

Gill, S. (2003). *Power and resistance in the new world order*. New York, NY: Palgrave Macmillan.

Gintis, H. (2000). Beyond *homo economicus*: Evidence from experimental economics. *Ecological Economics, 35*(3), 311–322.

Glick, P. (2005). Choice of scapegoats. In J. F. Dovidio, P. E. Glick, & L. A. Rudman (Eds.), *On the nature of prejudice: Fifty years after Allport* (pp. 244–261). Malden, MA: Blackwell.

Goatly, A. (2006). Humans, animals, and metaphors. *Society & Animals, 14*(1), 15–37.

Gould, S. J. (1993). American polygeny and craniometry before Darwin: Blacks and Indians as separate, inferior species. In S. Harding (Ed.), *The "racial" economy of science* (pp. 84–115). Bloomington, IN: Indiana University Press.

Gould, S. J. (1996). *The mismeasure of man* (Rev. ed.). New York, NY: W. W. Norton & Co.

Hiebert, T. (1996). Rethinking dominion theology. *Direction Journal, 25*(2), 16–25.

Hughes, J. D. (1975). *Ecology in ancient civilization*. Albuquerque, NM: University of New Mexico Press.

Hursh, D. (2005). Neo-liberalism, markets and accountability: Transforming education and undermining democracy in the United States and England. *Policy Futures in Education, 3*(1), 3–15. doi:10.2304/pfie.2005.3.1.6

The Interfaith Center for Sustainable Development. (2017). *Holy land seminarians faith and ecology project*. Retrieved from http://www.interfaithsustain.com/holy-land-faith-leaders

Kennedy, R. F. (1968, March 18). *Remarks at the University of Kansas*. Retrieved from https://www.jfklibrary.org/Research/Research-Aids/Ready-Reference/RFK-

Speeches/Remarks-of-Robert-F-Kennedy-at-the-University-of-Kansas-March-18-1968.aspx

Kiely, R. (2007). *The new political economy of development: Globalization, imperialism, hegemony.* New York, NY: Palgrave Macmillan.

Kraus, M. W., Côté, S., & Keltner, D. (2010). Social class, contextualism, and empathic accuracy. *Psychological Science, 21*(11), 1716–1723. doi:10.1177/0956797610387613

Kuznets, S. (1934). *National income, 1929–1932* (Senate Report No. 124). Washington, DC: U.S. Government Printing Office.

Ladson-Billings, G. (1998). Just what is critical race theory and what's it doing in a nice field like education? *International Journal of Qualitative Studies in Education, 11*(1), 7–24.

Leonard, T. C. (2009). Origins of the myth of social Darwinism: The ambiguous legacy of Richard Hofstadter's *Social Darwinism in American thought. Journal of Economic Behavior & Organization, 71*(1), 37–51.

Linning, S. (2014, December 27). Who said crime doesn't pay? Counting prostitution and drugs in the GDP figure has seen the UK's economy overtake France as fifth largest in the world. *MailOnline.* Retrieved from http://www.dailymail.co.uk/news/article-2888416/Who-said-crime-doesn-t-pay-Counting-prostitution-drugs-GDP-figure-seen-UK-s-economy-overtake-France-fifth-largest-world.html

Locke, J. (1689). *Two treatises of government.* London, UK: Awnsham Churchill.

Lomborg, B. (2001). *The skeptical environmentalist: Measuring the real state of the world.* New York, NY: Cambridge University Press.

Malthus, T. (1789). *An essay on the principle of population as it affects the future improvement of society, with remarks on the speculations of Mr. Goodwin, M. Condorcet and other writers.* London, UK: J. Johnson.

Malthus, T. (1803). *An essay on the principle of population* (2nd ed.). London, UK: J.M. Dent.

McKibben, B. (2007). *Deep economy: The wealth of communities and the durable future.* New York, NY: H. Holt & Co.

McMichael, P. (2012). *Development and social change: A global perspective.* Thousand Oaks, CA: Sage.

Merchant, C. (2001). Dominion over nature. In I. Bartsch & M. Lederman (Eds.), *The gender and science reader* (pp. 68–81). New York, NY: Routledge.

Monbiot, G. (2016, April 15). Neoliberalism: The ideology at the root of all our problems. *The Guardian.* Retrieved from https://www.theguardian.com/books/2016/apr/15/neoliberalism-ideology-problem-george-monbiot

Moore Lappé, F. (1971). *Diet for a small planet.* New York, NY: Ballantine Books.

Murray, A. (2017, June 2). Why business opposes Trump's retreat from Paris climate pact. *Fortune.* Retrieved from http://fortune.com/2017/06/02/paris-climate-withdrawal-trump-business

Mykleby, M., & Porter, W. (2011). *A national strategic narrative.* Washington, DC: Woodrow Institute for International Scholars.

Nef, J. U. (1977). An early energy crisis and its consequences. *Scientific American, 237*(5), 140–151.

Rolt, L. T. C., & Allen, J. S. (1977). *The steam engine of Thomas Newcomen.* Totnes, Devon: Moorland Publishing.

Ryan, W. (1972). *Blaming the victim.* New York, NY: Vintage.

Said, E. (1998). *Culture and imperialism.* New York, NY: Vintage Books.

Simon, J. (1996). *The ultimate resource 2.* Princeton, NJ: Princeton University Press.

Smith, B. D. (1998). *The emergence of agriculture*. New York, NY: Scientific American Library.

Stellar, J. E., Manzo, V. M., Kraus, M. W., & Keltner, D. (2012). Class and compassion: Socioeconomic factors predict responses to suffering. *Emotion, 12*(3), 449–459.

Thacker, S. C. (1999). NAFTA coalitions and the political viability of neoliberalism in Mexico. *Journal of Interamerican Studies and World Affairs, 41*(2), 57–89.

Thaler, R. H. (2000). From homo economicus to homo sapiens. *The Journal of Economic Perspectives, 14*(1), 133–141.

Truman, H. S. (1949, January 20). Inaugural address. Retrieved from *The American Presidency Project* website: http://www.presidency.ucsb.edu/ws/?pid=13282

Whelan, J. (2002). Lies, damn lies and statistics: Musings of a skeptical environmental educator. *Applied Environmental Education and Communication, 1*(3): 149–151.

White, Jr., L. (1967). The historical roots of our ecological crisis. *Science, 155*(3767), 1203–1207.

Wood, E. M. (2002). *The origin of capitalism: A longer view* (2nd ed.). London, UK: Verso.

Woodburn, J. (1982). Egalitarian societies. *Man, 17*(3), 431–451.

3

A DIFFERENT NARRATIVE

The Story of Better

In the iconic 1939 film *The Wizard of Oz*, Dorothy, a Kansas farm girl, gets swept up in a tornado that plunks her down in the fantastical, full-color world of Oz. Clutching her dog Toto, Dorothy looks around in wide-eyed wonder and declares, "I don't think we're in Kansas anymore."

That's how Moore, our character from the Story of More, will feel upon waking up in this chapter, the Story of Better. Transplanted into this topsy-turvy tale, Moore will encounter characters never before noticed and interact with the setting in a whole new way. The confounding developments will upend assumptions at every turn, making the Story of Better as strange to Moore as Oz appeared to Dorothy. Like Moore, you'll bump up against different ways of thinking, and as you compare the narratives of More and Better, you'll start pinpointing how they manifest in your curriculum. As we did in the last chapter, let's use questions as our signposts:

1. What's this story about?
2. Who are the characters and what are their motivations?
3. How do the characters and setting interact?
4. How do we know this narrative isn't some eco-fantasy?
5. How do the characters know whether they're on the right track?
6. How did this story get started?
7. As educators, where will we take the story?

What's This Story About?

In Chapter 1, we asked, *What do we need to thrive?* and responded with an ambitious list that included healthy and affordable food, strong relationships, and quality education. That's what the Story of Better is about—specifically, the mindsets and practices that can help us achieve these goals. Let's begin with an exercise that will refresh our thinking about *quantity* and *quality*, concepts introduced in the prior chapters.

Directions:

1. Fold a piece of paper in half. Label the left side "Things I value" and the right side "Expensive things that I have or would like to have."
2. Write down at least three responses for each side. Are there any items on both sides?
3. Look at your responses for "Things I value." Do any of them describe an experience that cost little or nothing but brought you great happiness or satisfaction? If not, can you think of such an experience?
4. Is the fulfillment you receive from your material possessions relative to the amount of time and money you spent to get them?

This activity differentiates *price*, which is quantitative; and *value*, which refers to qualitative benefits. Of course, the two are not mutually exclusive. For example, perhaps you identified a house or a college education as an "expensive" item. But I would also venture to guess that you greatly value the home you've made and the benefits of your education. Thus, as we travel through this chapter, let's keep in mind that the Story of Better does not demonize money; rather, it elevates the things, experiences, and relationships that truly improve our lives, whether or not there's a price attached. This reflects research findings about the correlation between income and happiness: The two rise together, but only up to a point (Easterlin, 2001).

Who Are the Characters and What Are Their Motivations?

In our last chapter, Moore enacted the role of the rugged individualist. While Moore was surrounded by a host of other characters—from individuals to nations—the winner-take-all competition that drove the story turned them into adversarial Others. So imagine the surprise when Moore suddenly realizes that not only does everyone count, but also everyone's well-being is actually connected.

The premise that we thrive when we abide *with* rather than *over* others is grounded in community and interdependence, concepts introduced in Chapter 1. These concepts redefine who and what counts as a character. In the Story of Better, significant actors include not only people but other species and ecosystems. Bringing nature from the background to the foreground also blurs the line between character and setting. The environment, which once served Moore's every whim, is now a cast of coactors that sustain the story. Moore even senses a biological affinity to nature—a psychological and emotional attachment believed to be a product of evolution (Kellert & Wilson,

1995). Known as *biophilia*, this trait only further changes our relationships with other species. In this narrative, humans are understood to be animals, infusing a sense of kinship that encourages respect and even a humbling recognition of similarities, such as the fact that we share 98% of our DNA with chimpanzees (Wildman, Uddin, Liu, Grossman, & Goodman, 2003). It also occurs to Moore that other species can be a source of learning and inspiration. This is the principle behind *biomimicry* a design and engineering field that emulates (rather than subjugates) the solutions nature has developed over billions of year (Benyus, 2002). For example, termite mounds stay cool in the desert, offering architects insights into how to design buildings for hot climates.

How Do the Characters and Setting Interact?

In the Story of Better, interdependence is the primary mode of interaction because the narrative derives from systems thinking, which emphasizes wholeness and connections rather than the reductionist worldview we saw in Chapter 2 (Meadows, 2008). It's all about relationships. But because some of them are hidden, let's bring them to the surface with the following activity.

Activity 3.1: Getting What We Need

Directions:

1. The top row of Table 3.1 shows a variety of ways we might obtain food, water, education, or other components of thriving shown in the left column. Recreate the table and add your own items to the left column.
2. For each item, put your initials in the column that describes how you get it. Are there any methods of obtaining needs you hadn't thought about before?
3. What could we learn from our students' responses if they were to complete this exercise?

TABLE 3.1 How Do We Get What We Need?

Item	I get this from family/ friends	I get this from nature	I get this at school	I get this in the community	I can make or grow this	I can buy this with money	I get this another way	I do not have a way to get this
Healthy food								
Water								
Education								

Source: Copyright 2009. Creative Change Educational Solutions. Used with permission.

This activity illustrates some of the relationships that the Story of More ignores, discounts, or subordinates. In that story line, relationships are forged primarily through markets; people are insatiable consumers who buy goods and services from producers. (You'll find these concepts in elementary social studies curricula.) But in the Story of Better, people engage in "transactions" among nature, family, friends, the larger community, and markets (Shiva, 2005). Here, we move among overlapping ecological, social, and cultural communities in our roles as family members, neighbors, and citizens—not simply consumers — even though we're likely to play that role as well. Moreover, businesses and people are not the only producers; the environment provides ecosystem services that maintain life for all.

Self in Community

At this point in the story, Moore is barely hanging on, grappling with the contours of an inconceivable world: a cast of thousands, a setting without boundaries, and the startling realization that we're all in this together. The script contradicts the Story of More in practically every way. Moore's no longer the center of the world, raising a disquieting question: "Do I even count?" Rest assured the answer is yes, although the concept of self is based on a fundamentally different understanding of human nature.

In the Story of More, *homo economicus* was driven by self-interest, a motivation presumed to be a "transhistorical attribute" of humans (McMichael, 2012, p. 5). But the Story of Better foregrounds other innate traits such as empathy, cooperation, and altruistic behavior (Sober & Wilson, 1999). So does that mean Moore's individuality doesn't matter anymore?

Hardly.

The Story of Better only works if characters are granted human dignity within community. Self and society are thus mutually supporting: Strong communities are the fruit of individuals who are both "self-determining (able to develop their full capacities)" and responsible "toward and with others, their society, the environment, and the broader world in which we live" (Adams & Bell, 2016, p. 3). Situating our individuality within a social context spreads benefits all around. A visit to my local farmers market means quality food for me and revenue for the local economy. Likewise, teachers who develop each student's individual potential create conditions for democratic classrooms where everyone contributes.

The Tragedy of the Commons

Social accountability also informs codes of conduct for maintaining the Commons. Recall that in Chapter 1, Hardin (1968) asserted that open-access resources (e.g., pastures) are doomed to be overused, with privatization as one remedy. In Chapter 2, we saw a historical example of privatizing pastures in

England. But enclosing resources doesn't necessarily provide fair access to everyone, and that's why this chapter, "The Story of Better," offers other possibilities for managing the Commons.

In this story, shared resources are not an inevitable calamity, but rather the physical and cultural manifestation of our interdependence. In the Story of Better, management strategies weigh private gain with public needs, gauge long- and short-term impacts, and include the voices of all affected. Elinor Ostrom (1933–2012), the only woman to win the Nobel Prize in economics, researched cultures around the globe to identify the practices and institutions that contribute to maintaining the Commons (Dietz, Ostrom, & Stern, 2003; Ostrom 1990). Here are some of the favorable conditions:

- All who depend on the resource can access it.
- Stakeholders—individuals, communities, local organizations, governments—use democratic processes to make decisions and settle conflict.
- Resource boundaries are defined through community agreements, public management, cultural norms, private property rights, or other means that include mechanisms to hold users accountable.
- People recognize that individual actions impact and occur within larger social and ecological systems.
- Benefits and costs are equitably shared (not necessarily *equally*, i.e., in even portions).
- Local communities are empowered, not marginalized.

The research of Dietz and his colleagues (2003) revealed that cultures can *choose* to base decisions on equity, interdependence, and mutual accountability. This reality unseats the profits-first account of human nature, which Polanyi (1944) argued is a notion specific to modern capitalism. That said, the potential for cooperative behavior does not mean that competition simply evaporates from the Story of Better. However, it takes on a different form than the winner-take-all version we've discussed.

The term *competition* derives from the Latin *competere*, meaning "to strive for." This begs the question, "What are we striving for and how will we get it?" (Santone, 2016). Labor scholar David Reynolds (2002) distinguished between "low road" and "high road" competition. The former is a zero-sum approach that, like the Gross Domestic Product (GDP), externalizes social and environmental costs. In contrast, high road competition encourages a quest for excellence in a fair rivalry. Making a connection to athletics, a physical education teacher framed competition as an honest contest between skilled players; that is, may the best, not the most ruthless, win. A retired Marine Corps drill sergeant, the teacher also brought in the idea of competing against one's self to constantly strengthen the team—another example of how the well-being of individuals and communities support one another.

Zero-sum competition has also been challenged as a strategy for international relations, with a powerful critique coming from Captain Wayne Porter (U.S. Navy, retired) and Colonel Mark Mykleby (U.S. Marine Corps, retired); both men served in the Pentagon as strategic advisors to the former Chairman of the Joint Chiefs of Staff, Admiral Mike Mullen. Porter and Mykleby's (2011) treatise, *A National Strategic Narrative* (available online), called into question the Cold War paradigm of domination that positions other nations as adversaries. In its place, the authors make an inspiring case for a new story based on sustainable prosperity, global interdependence, and diplomacy. Declaring that "dominance, like fossil fuels, is not a sustainable form of power" (p. 5), the document advocated for a conception of national strength achieved through sustainability and investments in education, youth, and social services.

The nature of competition—and even the need for it—depends on what we're striving for. A rival resource such as land can engender a cooperative solution, a winner-take-all competition, or something in between (Dietz et al., 2013). However, nonrival assets such as respect or equality should generate no competition at all. In a democracy, there should be no reason to jockey for rights or respect because they are (theoretically) guaranteed to all. In Part II, we'll revisit this idea and its implications for classroom practice.

The Centrality of Diversity

In the Story of More, diversity presents a barrier to the uniformity and social order needed for control. But in the Story of Better, people value diversity not as a superficial quality to *celebrate,* but as a condition of life that is essential for sustaining the Commons.

In terms of human communities, characters in this story know that thriving depends on learning with, from, and about one another. People maintain or resurrect knowledge and traditions with proven value and wisdom, for example, tapping Inuit understanding of the Arctic to address climate change, or reviving farming practices that simultaneously support the health of people and the environment (Romig, Garlynd, Harris, & McSweeney, 1995). Likewise, in classrooms, students' cultures, families, and communities, history serve as valid and important sources of learning alongside "high status" academic knowledge (Apple, 1995, p. 13).

Honoring tradition does not imply that culture is static. On the contrary, change is expected, but the decision-making process is inclusive; people deliberately weight benefits, consequences, and their equitable distribution so that no single group is disproportionately privileged or burdened. Policies focus on preventing problems and finding alternatives to potentially harmful actions— two elements of the "precautionary principle" (Kriebel et al., 2001).

Diversity also has an ecological element that provides additional insights into competition. While species compete for food, habitat, and mates, ecological constraints create checks. Eliminating species weakens the system, whereas biodiversity helps buffer ecosystems against catastrophic changes that cross recovery thresholds (Thompson, Mackey, McNulty, & Mosseler, 2009). This has parallels in human societies. For example, economic diversification can reduce a community's vulnerability when a particular sector declines and jobs disappear due to, for example, the closing of a major factory. Diversity thus supports resiliency, the ability of a system to absorb and "bounce back" from disruptions (Lewis, 2011).

Discussion Questions

1. The text describes ways humans are motivated by self-interest as well as concern for the common good. What parallels can you draw to student motivation and incentives (overt or covert) offered by your school? For example, what individualized "rewards" drive your students? Are there group incentives that are motivating, such as a class party to celebrate successful completion of a challenging project? Which types of motivations are most effective?
2. What type(s) of diversity are discussed in your institution? Cultural? Linguistic? Biological? Socioeconomic? What are some of the scripts and narratives about these or other forms of diversity?

How Do We Know This Isn't Just Eco-fantasy?

At this point in the journey, Moore is starting to get on board and is especially relieved to know that individuality matters. But with all that diversity and community, Moore is thinking the story seems like a touchy-feely fantasy. Moreover, the very concept of interdependence is unsettling because it hooks Moore into relationships with inescapable obligations. Zero-sum competition is self-defeating—and that brings down the entire premise of the Story of Better, which Moore is so comfortable with. It's frightening to find cracks in your belief system, so Moore tries to dismiss the story as an extremist eco-ideology.

Whoa, Moore. Not so fast. Put tree-hugging out of your mind and consider something tangible and familiar: your everyday life. See whether you (and you, the reader) can complete these sentences:

*   The coffee at my school comes from _____.
*   Food waste at our school goes _____.
*   The electricity in my community comes from _____.
*   When I use fossil fuels, the emissions go _____.

These simple statements illustrate an irrefutable truth: Everything we use comes from somewhere in the environment (near or far), and all the wastes go back into it (also near and far).

This is not ideology. It's plain old science.

If science is not your field, don't worry—and don't skip ahead. The principles we'll introduce here are relevant to many disciplines and useful in our roles as educators and citizens. Here's a simple explanation of our reliance on the environment framed around the backstory of Moore's favorite food: French fries.

Growing the potato (a russet Burbank) requires sunlight and water from rainfall, groundwater, rivers, or irrigation systems. The potato also requires productive soil, perhaps nourished by manure, compost, and/or synthetic nitrogen fertilizers. Manufacturing the latter requires extracting nitrogen from the atmosphere, a process which itself is fueled by copious amounts of natural gas. Excess fertilizer can wash into streams, where the added nutrients induce the growth of plants and algae, which in turn can deplete oxygen for other species. Cutting and cooking the French fries requires machines, electricity, and labor. The fuel for that might come from petroleum or coal, and ... you get the picture.

This short example demonstrates that the economy is embedded within the larger environment (Daly & Farley, 2004). As stated, everything we use or create ultimately comes from the environment, and all wastes go back into it. An old tire might end up in a landfill. The gaseous wastes from fossil fuel combustion end up in the atmosphere or the ocean. Thus, it is impossible to throw something away because wastes stick around in one form or another. These basic scientific facts thoroughly trounce the myth peddled in the Story of More, that is, the environment is external and merely a jumble of disposable props that serve the real action: growth.

Now that we understand the fundamental relationships, the next question is, how do we know whether we're consuming resources in ways that the environment can support? Daly (1980) posited that human activity is within the earth's limits if it meets these conditions:

1. Renewable resources are used within rates of regeneration (e.g., fish are harvested at rates of repopulation).
2. Polluting wastes, if discharged into the environment (ideally they wouldn't be), are released at a level and rate that nature can process (e.g., nitrogen fertilizer enters waterways at a level and rate that plants and wetlands can purify).
3. Society transitions away from nonrenewable resources (e.g., fossil fuels) at a pace that allows a smooth transition to renewable sources such as solar or wind energy.

In short, the environment is a complex and wondrous system capable of regeneration and self-cleansing—but within limits.

These ecological and physical constraints are real, but narratives determine whether or not we accept and respect them (Bowers, 2002). Disconnected from the larger environment, the Story of More spins the fantasy that unlimited growth is possible. In contrast, the Story of Better recognizes that the world has constraints and that there are consequences for pretending otherwise.

Discussion Questions

1. What concepts or principles from your discipline can help us understand the principles illustrated in the preceding section?
2. Tracing the life story of a product, that is, life cycle analysis, is an effective way to teach about the often hidden ways we're connected to the environment; we used French fries as our example. Considering the age of your students and your discipline, what would be an item with a life cycle that students could understand? For example, young children could trace how a strawberry from a nearby garden becomes jam given the immediate and tangible steps (growth, cooking, consumption). Students ready for a far-flung geographical and temporal backstory can tackle items such as a cell phone, which relies on materials and labor from multiple continents for both manufacturing and disposal.

How Do the Characters Know Whether They're Successful?

At long last, Moore is starting to warm up. Individual well-being still matters, money and *stuff* have a role, and that fries-and-science thing was pretty mind-blowing. Maybe this story isn't so outlandish after all. But with so many nonlinear plot lines, Moore is not sure how to gauge progress. Let's help Moore out by looking at two important metrics: the Genuine Progress Indicator (GPI) and the Ecological Footprint (EF).

The Genuine Progress Indicator

Recall that the Story of More's core indicator was the GDP, a straightforward measurement of the exchange of money. The Story of Better uses an adapted alternative, the GPI; (Daly & Cobb, 1989; Talberth, Cobb, & Slattery, 2007). Like the GDP, the GPI includes all expenditures. However, unlike the GDP, the GPI adds the value of *positives* such as volunteer work and subtracts the costs of *negatives* such as pollution (Talberth & Weisdorf, 2017). For example, based on factors such as health costs, Talberth and Weisdorf calculated that pollution costs society $3,714.65 per capita per year; this figure would be subtracted from the GDP to reflect the detrimental impacts, providing a clearer picture of well-being.

The GPI's *full cost* approach also changes the definition of *cheap*. Consider two bags of coffee; coffee A is grown in ways that contribute to deforestation, while coffee B is grown with methods that preserve biodiversity. The price tag of coffee A is lower than coffee B's, but only because the costs associated with habitat destruction and soil erosion are not factored in. Conversely, coffee B now appears quite economical when we consider the free services provided by biodiversity, such as natural pest control. This comparison of price and full cost can also be applied to labor practices, transportation, and other factors in the coffees' back stories.

The methodologies used to calculate the GPI are evolving and often debated.[1] Nonetheless, the GPI makes significant steps toward correcting the misleading picture of well-being that arises from the GDP's cherry-picked calculations. And, the use of the GPI and related metrics has been gaining ground at the national, regional, and city levels around the world (Talberth & Weisdorf, 2017). For example, the country of Bhutan has adopted a "Gross National Happiness Index" that considers nine domains, including psychological well-being, cultural diversity, ecological resilience, and education (Ura, Alkire, Zangmo, & Wangdi, 2012).

The EF: Measuring Our Impact

We've learned that human activity is embedded within and constrained by the environment. This means we must scale human consumption to ecological limits. But with more than 7 billion people, how can we even begin to measure the impact of human consumption? Let's shrink it down to your everyday life, just as we did before. Consider the following:

- How many trees would it take to provide all of the paper you use in a year or absorb the greenhouse gas emissions you create?
- How many acres of cropland does it take to feed you for a year?
- How much landfill space would it take to hold your garbage?

The answer to these questions is your EF, a measurement of the amount of resources an individual or population requires to (a) produce everything it consumes, and (b) absorb all its wastes (Global Footprint Network [GFN], 2012). The EF's peer-reviewed calculations start with a baseline measure of *bioproductive* land: forests, croplands, grazing lands, fishing grounds, and other areas that support life for all species (Wackernagel et al., 2002). There are about 12 billion hectares (30 billion acres) of bioproductive land, but humanity is consuming the equivalent of 48 billion acres (the equivalent of 1.6 earths; World Wildlife Fund, 2016).

But how can this be if there is only one planet? The 0.6 represents *overshoot,* that is, exceeding the limits on what the earth can provide. Overshoot means we are harvesting renewable resources faster than they can replenish and putting more wastes into the environment than it can absorb and process—two warning signs of ecological unsustainability we reviewed earlier. Placing this stress on the earth's ecosystems damages their ability to replenish. Mathis Wackernagel, a founder of EF methodology, explained this using the metaphor of a bank account (Wackernagel, White, & Moran, 2004). Think of the 30 billion acres of bioproductive land as the principle (the account balance) and environmental regeneration as the interest. To maintain the balance, we need to live within our means and accrue interest; but instead, humans are overdrawing the principle. Moderate UN projections suggest that if current population and consumption trends continue, we will need the equivalent of two earths by 2030. But when it comes to land, as Mark Twain once quipped, "They're not making it anymore."

At the individual level, footprint size varies depending on factors such as use of technology, energy, transportation, the type of diet and housing.[2] Not surprisingly, the average per capita footprint in industrialized nations is significantly higher than that in nonindustrialized ones. For example, the average footprint of a U.S. citizen is about 8.2 hectares (about 23 acres). Denmark comes in at 5.5 hectares, Costa Rica at 2.8, and Kenya at 1 (Global Footprint Network [GFN], 2017). These are simply averages and do not reflect individual differences within a country.

Right-sizing EF to global biocapacity is needed to sustain the environment. However, the question is not simply, *How do we get the lowest footprint?* After all, we could drastically reduce our footprint by not eating or not having a home. But deprivation is not the goal. Rather, the real question is, *How can communities thrive while sustaining the environmental systems they're a part of?*

Where Did the Story Come From?

Throughout history, the Story of Better's teachings are found across religious traditions and associated cultures (Oldfield & Alcom, 1991). To parallel the discussion of religion from Chapter 2, let's take a quick tour of some key teachings from various faiths (in alphabetical order).

- Buddhism: This faith is grounded in the interdependence of all beings through cycles of birth, suffering, death, and rebirth (*samsara*; Swearer, 1998). Buddhism's contemporary leader, the Dalai Lama, emphasized our shared responsibility to address today's problems: "The world grows ... more and more interdependent ... today more than ever before life must be characterized by a sense of universal responsibility, not only ... human to human but also human to other forms of life" (cited in Swearer, 1998, para. 17).
- Christianity: Environmental teachings and theology appear across many Christian denominations under a range of frameworks, including creation spirituality and Christian stewardship (Ellingson, Woodley, & Paik, 2012). Driven by a shared responsibility to care for (not worship) the earth, multidenominational organizations such as Interfaith Power and Light are promoting energy conservation efforts, such as the installation of solar panels on houses of worship (Fair, 2017).

- For Catholics, Pope Francis (elected 2013) has been a vocal advocate for environmental stewardship and care for the poor, two pillars of Catholic Social Teachings. His 2015 Encyclical Letter, *Laudato Si*, elevated the moral imperative to simultaneously confront climate change and poverty. Referring to the earth as both a sister and mother, he stated, "We have come to see ourselves as her lords and masters, entitled to plunder her at our will" (p. 3), and then details the "tragic effects ... on the world's poorest" (p. 12).
- Islam: The concept of stewardship (*khilafa*) is based on the obligation to serve Allah and care for his creation as "a beneficiary and not a disposer" (Arab News, 2014, para. 20). With much of the Islamic world already hard-hit by droughts and extreme heat, movements such as "green Islam" or "eco-Islam" are elevating *khilafa* as "an inherent Muslim necessity" (Zbidi, 2013, para. 6). The Global Muslim Climate Network, a coalition that includes scholars and nongovernmental organizations, has called upon Muslim nations to increase the use of renewable energy. For example, Morocco has launched national efforts to retrofit 15,000 mosques with solar panels and energy-saving technologies (Greene, 2017).
- Judaism: The Judaic concept of *tikkun olam*, "'mending' or 'improving' the world," expresses the belief in one's moral obligation to the larger society (Shatz, Waxman, & Diament, 1997, p. 1). Environmentally, this encompasses "repairing what we have polluted" (Dorff, 2007, p. 3). To emphasize humility among other species, an unnamed Rabbi wryly observed that "Adam was created at the end of the sixth day so that if human beings should grow too arrogant, they may be reminded that even the gnats preceded them in the order of creation" (cited in Fink, 2004, p. 231).
- Native American beliefs: Indigenous religions are often held up as belief systems grounded in interdependence, reciprocity, and the concept of the earth as a living being (Booth & Jacobs, 1990). The view that humans are one part of the larger world is perfectly expressed by Luther Standing Bear, a Lakota writer, in his 1933 work, *Land of the Spotted Eagle*: "Man did not occupy a special place in the eyes of Wakan Tanka, the Grandfather of us all. I was only a part of everything that was called the world" (cited in Grim, 2004, para. 5).

Of course, religions are not monolithic; beliefs and practices vary within and across denominations. For example, many evangelical Christians deny climate change or humans' role in it (Funk & Alper, 2015). Proponents of this view argue that humans simply don't have the power to influence the earth's climate and that God will intervene if it comes to that. Lawmakers are carrying this view into policy discussions. For example, in a town hall meeting, Tim Walberg (R–Michigan) said, "I'm confident that, if there's a real problem, he [sic] can take care of it" (cited in Vox, 2017, para. 2).

Discussion Questions

1. If you practice a particular faith or identify as spiritual (if not religious), how have the teachings of your religion or your spirituality informed your thinking about the environment?
2. What similarities and differences are there among the teachings from different faiths? If applicable, bring in your knowledge and experiences outside of this text.
3. Suppose Moore insists that regardless of interdependence, the environment exists to serve people. Do you think you could get Moore on board with (for example) energy conservation initiatives? How would you make your case?

As Educators, Where Will We Take the Story?

While we've touched upon educational connections in Part I, Part II will explicitly focus on ways the stories of More and Better run parallel in curriculum, pedagogy, and our beliefs about students. This progression will equip you to unearth mindsets and practices that may be holding students back from reaching their potential; along the way, you'll explore ideas for curriculum adaptations. In preparation, the Part I Culminating Activity will help you reflect upon the concepts we've covered and identify those most relevant to your teaching. Later, in Part III, you'll return to these concepts and apply them to your curriculum.

After surviving harrowing perils in Oz, Dorothy is anxious to return home and pleads her case before the apparition of the "great and mighty" Wizard of Oz. Toto, her trusty dog, leaps from her arms and pulls back a nearby curtain, revealing the sorcerer to be an ordinary man creating hocus-pocus with light and sound. The man urges Dorothy to "pay no attention," but it's too late. Dorothy's seen the chicanery, freeing her from his power. Like Dorothy, you've also unmasked a formidable illusion: the inevitability of social inequities and environmental degradation.

And what of Moore? Imagine your students, colleagues—and even yourself—as Moore and Friends: earnest characters navigating confounding stories in the quest to write their own. We've seen that we *can* redirect the plot toward our desired future. But the question is, will we?

Sharpen your pencils and let's give it our best shot.

Notes

1 Readers interested in the GPI's methodology may consult the literature in the field of ecological economics.
2 You can measure your footprint at www.myfootprint.org.

References

Adams, M., & Bell, L. A. (Eds.). (2016). *Teaching for diversity and social justice* (3rd ed.). Abingdon, UK: Routledge.

Apple, M. W. (1995). The case for democratic schools. In M. Apple & J. A. Beane. (Eds). *Democratic schools* (pp. 1–25). Alexandria, VA: Association for Supervision & Curriculum Development.

Arab News. (2014, January 17). *Protection of environment is the duty of every Muslim*. Retrieved from http://www.arabnews.com/news/510411

Benyus, J. M. (2002). *Biomimicry: Innovation inspired by nature*. New York, NY: William Morrow Paperbacks.

Booth, A. L., & Jacobs, H. M. (1990). Ties that bind: Native American beliefs as a foundation for environmental consciousness. *Environmental Ethics, 12*(1), 27–43.

Bowers, C. A. (2002), Toward an eco-justice pedagogy. *Environmental Education Research, 8*(1), 21–34.

Daly, H. (Ed.). (1980). *Economics, ecology, ethics: Essays toward a steady-state economy*. San Francisco, CA: W.H. Freeman.

Daly, H., & Cobb, J. (1989). *For the common good: Redirecting the economy toward community, the environment, and a sustainable future*. Boston, MA: Beacon Press.

Daly, H. E., & Farley, J. (2004). *Ecological economics: Principles and applications*. Washington, DC: Island Press.

Dietz, T., Ostrom, E., & Stern, P. C. (2003). The struggle to govern the commons. *Science, 302*(5652), 1907–1912.

Dorff, E. N. (2007). *The way into tikkun olam (repairing the world)*. Woodstock, VT: Jewish Lights Publishing.

Easterlin, R. A. (2001). Income and happiness: Towards a unified theory. *The Economic Journal, 111*(473), 465–484.

Ellingson, S., Woodley, V. A., & Paik, A. (2012). The structure of religious environmentalism: Movement organizations, interorganizational networks, and collective action. *Journal for the Scientific Study of Religion, 51*(2), 266–285. doi:10.1111/j.1468-5906.2012.01639

Fair, D. (2017, July 19). Issues of the environment: Ann Arbor partners-up to get houses of worship to "go solar." *WEMU 89.1*. Retrieved from http://wemu.org/post/issues-environment-ann-arbor-partners-get-houses-worship-go-solar

Fink, G. (2004). Growing up Jewish in Ferrara: The fiction of Giorgio Bassani, a personal recollection. *Judaism: A Quarterly Journal of Jewish Life and Thought, 53*(3–4), 293–300.

Funk, C., & Alper, B. A. (2015, October). Religion and views on climate and energy issues. In *Religion and science: Highly religious Americans are less likely than others to see conflict between faith and science* (pp. 32–41). Washington, DC: Pew Research Center.

Global Footprint Network. (2012). How the footprint works. Retrieved from https://www.footprintnetwork.org/our-work/ecological-footprint

Greene, E. (2017). Muslim activists build bridges. *Green America*. Retrieved from https://www.greenamerica.org/economic-action-against-hate/muslim-activists-build-bridges

Grim, J. A. (2004). *Indigenous traditions and ecology*. New Haven, CT: The Forum on Religion and Ecology at Yale. Retrieved from http://fore.research.yale.edu/religion/indigenous/index.html

Hardin, G. (1968). The tragedy of the commons. *Science, 162*(3859), 1243–1248.

Kellert, S. R., & Wilson, E. O. (Eds.). (1995). *The biophilia hypothesis*. Washington, DC: Island Press.

Kriebel, D., Tickner, J., Epstein, P., Lemons, J., Levins, R., Loechler, E. L., ... Stoto, M. (2001). The precautionary principle in environmental science. *Environmental Health Perspectives, 109*(9), 871–876.

Lewis, T. G. (2011). *Bak's sand pile: Strategies for a catastrophic world*. Williams, CA: Agile Press.

McMichael, P. (2012). *Development and social change: A global perspective*. Thousand Oaks, CA: Sage.

Meadows, D. H. (2008). *Thinking in systems: A primer*. White River Junction, VT: Chelsea Green.

Oldfield, M. L., & Alcom, J. B. (Eds.). (1991). *Biodiversity: Culture, conservation, and ecodevelopment*. Boulder, CO: Westview Press.

Ostrom, E. (1990). *Governing the commons*. Cambridge, UK: Cambridge University Press.

Polanyi, K. (1944). *The great transformation: The political and economic origin of our time*. Boston, MA: Beacon Press.

Porter, W., & Mykleby, M. (2011). *A national strategic narrative*. Washington, DC: Woodrow Wilson International Center for Scholars.

Reynolds, D. B. (2002). *Taking the high road: Communities organize for economic change*. Armonk, NY: ME Sharpe.

Romig, D. E., Garlynd, M. J., Harris, R. F., & McSweeney, K. (1995). How farmers assess soil health and quality. *Journal of Soil and Water Conservation, 50*(3), 229–236.

Santone, S. (2016). Beyond neoliberalism: Education for sustainable development and a new paradigm of global cooperation. In R. Papa & A. Saiti (Eds.), *Building for a sustainable future in our schools: Brick by brick* (pp. 62–84). New York, NY: Springer.

Shatz, D., Waxman, C. I., & Diament, N. J. (Eds.). (1997). *Tikkun olam: Social responsibility in Jewish thought and law*. Lanham, MD: Rowman & Littlefield.

Shiva, V. (2005). *Earth democracy: Justice, sustainability, and peace*. Berkeley, CA: North Atlantic Books.

Sober, E., & Wilson, D. S. (1999). *Unto others: The evolution and psychology of unselfish behavior*. Cambridge, MA: Harvard University Press.

Swearer, D. K. (1998). Buddhism and ecology: Challenge and promise. *Earth Ethics, 10*(1), 19–22.

Talberth, J., Cobb, C., & Slattery, N. (2007). *The genuine progress indicator 2006 : A tool for sustainable development*. Oakland, CA: Redefining Progress.

Talberth, J., & Weisdorf, M. (2017). Genuine progress indicator 2.0: Pilot accounts for the US, Maryland, and City of Baltimore 2012–2014. *Ecological Economics, 142*(1), 1–11.

Thompson, I., Mackey, B., McNulty, S., & Mosseler, A. (2009). *Forest resilience, biodiversity, and climate change: A synthesis of the biodiversity/resilience/stability relationship in forest ecosystems* (CBD Technical Series No. 43). Montreal, Quebec, CA: Secretariat of the Convention on Biological Diversity.

Ura, K., Alkire, S., Zangmo, T., & Wangdi, K. (2012). *A short guide to gross national happiness index*. Thimphu, Bhutan: The Centre for Bhutan Studies.

Vox, L. (2017, June 2). Why don't Christian conservatives worry about climate change? God. *The Washington Post*. Retrieved from https://www.washingtonpost.com/posteverything/wp/2017/06/02/why-dont-christian-conservatives-worry-about-climate-change-god/?utm_term=.a891c5cf8da1

Wackernagel, M., Schulz, N. B., Deumling, D., Linares, A. C., Jenkins, M., Kapos, V., ... Randers, J. (2002). Tracking the ecological overshoot of the human economy. *Proceedings of the National Academy of Sciences, 99*(14), 9266–9271. Retrieved from http://www.pnas.org/content/99/14/9266.full.pdf

Wackernagel, M., White, S., & Moran, D. (2004). Using ecological footprint accounts: From analysis to applications. *International Journal of Environment and Sustainable Development, 3*(3–4), 293–315.

Wildman, D. E., Uddin, M., Liu, G., Grossman, L. I., & Goodman, M. (2003). Implications of natural selection in shaping 99.4% nonsynonymous DNA identity between humans and chimpanzees: Enlarging genus *Homo. Proceedings of the National Academy of Sciences, 100*(12), 7181–7188.

World Wildlife Fund. (2016). *Living planet report 2016: Summary.* Gland, Switzerland: WWF International.

Zbidi, M. (2013). The call to eco-jihad. *Islamic environmentalism.* Retrieved from https://en.qantara.de/content/islamic-environmentalism-the-call-to-eco-jihad

PART I

Culminating Activity
Defining Sustainability and Social Justice

Chapters 1–3 gave us a broad look at the underlying forces affecting progress toward sustainability and social justice. Here, we'll review core ideas and apply them to formally define the two terms. It's trickier than grabbing a dictionary, so let's start with some background.

What Is Sustainability?

The terms *sustainability* and *sustainable* are increasingly used in common parlance in reference to everything from locally sourced food to recycling (among the most common associations). But it's this very popularity that's fueling misuse and confusion.

Perhaps the most problematic use of "sustainable" is in the context of business, where the term is typically paired with *growth* and *profits.* These usages are contradictory because we know that material output is constrained by environmental limits. "Sustainable growth" is thus an oxymoron (Daly, 1996). That said, it all depends on what's growing. An increase in happiness, health, and access to healthy food provides us with both *more* and *better,* as we've explored.

At the global level, the phrase *sustainable development* gained prominence with the 1987 publication of *Our Common Future,* a landmark report by the World Commission on Environment and Development (WCED). Also known as the Brundtland Report, the document highlighted the often-cited three Es of sustainability: **e**nvironmental regeneration and stewardship, **e**conomic prosperity, and **e**quitable societies.

The Brundtland Report also coined a much-quoted definition of sustainable development: meeting the needs of the present without compromising the ability of future generations to meet their needs (WCED, 1987). However, some scholars have bristled at the term "development" because of its historic association with colonialism (Feinstein, 2009). Still other critiques have noted that the report's call for a "new era of economic growth" (WCED, 1987, p. 1) merely perpetuates the anthropocentrism in the Story of More (Jickling, 2001; Sneddon, Howarth, & Norgaard, 2006).

Sustainability has also been described as "balancing" the three Es, with the overlap shown in Figure I.1. While this concept is easy to grasp, it suggests that the three Es come together in small ways, with each E operating more or less independently.

The concentric circles view of sustainability presented in Figure I.2 more accurately illustrates what we have learned about nested systems: (a) the environment is the containing system, (b) human societies and cultures exist within

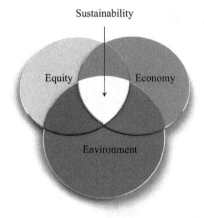

FIGURE I.1 The Three "E" View of Sustainability.

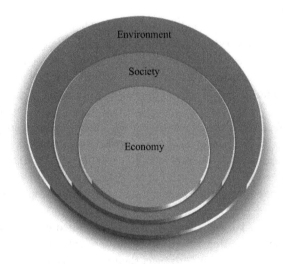

FIGURE I.2 The Nested Systems View of Sustainability.

that, and (c) economic structures are products of those societies. The overlapping lines in Figure I.1 represent the permeability among the three dimensions.

This systems view of the world lends itself to this definition of sustainability: Enabling all (species) to thrive, now and into the future, in an equitable way, within the means of the environment (Agyeman, Bullard, & Evans, 2003).

Sustainability can be interpreted in many different ways, and to ensure the term is meaningful to your work, let's derive a relevant definition based on the ideas from Part I.

Directions:

1. Flip back through Chapters 1–3 and identify the passages or quotes that are most significant to you, your community, or your discipline. You can also draw from the concepts that follow, which were directly or indirectly addressed in the chapters. We'll refer to these terms as *foundational concepts*. In Parts II and III, you'll return to these concepts in the context of curriculum.
    *   **Beauty:** This quality enhances life and contributes to well-being.
    *   **Change:** Adaptation and evolution are conditions of life.
    *   **Community:** Humans are part of ecological, cultural, and social communities.
    *   **Diversity:** Biological, linguistic, and cultural diversities are connected and essential.
    *   **Ecological Health:** Regeneration of ecosystem services is essential for sustainability.
    *   **Equity:** Equal opportunity is the promise of democracy.
    *   **Ethics:** Ethics serve to guide human endeavor and is not just a topic for philosophy.
    *   **Interdependence:** The interconnectedness of human-environmental systems is a condition of life.
    *   **Limits/Scale:** Ecological limits and social ties should inform the scale of human activity.
    *   **Resilience:** Communities and their subsystems are stronger when they have the ability to absorb disruptions and bounce back.
    *   **Systems:** A system is an interdependent set of elements that form a complex whole.
    *   **Well-being:** Thriving (physical, ecological, etc.) is our goal.
2. Narrow your list of concepts to no more than five.
3. Create several sentences that integrate and distill your ideas. Following are a few that my students have come up with over the years. Sustainability is …
    *   considering everyone and everything to make the world better.
    *   how we want the world to be.
    *   well-being for all, today and in the future.

What Is Social Justice?

Like sustainability, *social justice* is a loaded term. An informal Google search yields a torrent of scornful blogs and videos mocking so-called snowflakes, safe spaces, political correctness, and all else disparaging of so-called "social justice warriors." I'm venturing a guess that the hysteria is intended to deflect attention away from oppression—the opposite of social justice. So let's start there.

Briefly, prejudice and bias are negative beliefs and attitudes, and stereotypes are simplistic generalizations. Prejudicial beliefs and stereotypes can lead to *discrimination,* the act of denying access to goods, resources, respect, and services to people based on their membership (real or perceived) in a particular social group (Stephan, 1999). *Oppression* goes beyond individual acts of discrimination and weaves it into the structures of everyday life, including schools, the judicial system, housing, and more. That's why we'll also use terms such as *institutional discrimination* to describe the structural, systemic barriers it presents.

Oppression is characterized by hierarchies of races, genders, and so forth, created and maintained by unequal distribution of power. Historically (and as this book will argue, at present), these hierarchies place, for example, Whites over people of color, and upper-class groups over other socioeconomic classes. Adams, Bell, & Griffin (1997) shed light on four ways oppression manifests itself among the dominant and nondominant groups in the hierarchy:

- The dominant group has the power to project its culture and norms so thoroughly that they become the prevailing definition of *regular* and *correct.*
- The hierarchy confers benefits and advantages to the dominant group, yet denies them to subordinate groups. Such inequality is *business as usual.*
- The dominant group misrepresents the subordinate group through, for example, stereotyping, distorting history, or stifling the voices that can threaten the arrangement or demand its restructuring.
- Members of the subordinate group may internalize the narratives of inferiority imposed by the dominant group (i.e., internalized oppression; Delgado, 1989; Ladson-Billings, 1998).

In short, oppression is "power + prejudice" in which dominant groups—consciously or unconsciously—enjoy advantages while subordinate groups are systematically disadvantaged.

Note the use of the word *group.* Oppressions distinguish between (a) individual acts of discrimination, and (b) unfair systems. While bigoted acts are of course wrong, oppression looks to the structural level. This brings us to another term: privilege.

Privilege refers to the unearned benefits the dominant group receives simply by being in the group. As Swalwell (2013) noted, privileged groups are "positioned by power relations within systems of supremacy … that are made stronger when rendered invisible, consciously or not, to those who benefit from them most" (pp. 5–6). Because individuals in the dominant group see their way as normal, they can easily stay blind to the structures that hold their position in place. Even privileged individuals who actively work against oppression reap the benefits. A White educator can devote a career to anti-racism, but is still unlikely to be pulled over, followed in a store, denied a loan, or assumed to be less capable due to skin color. Thus, privilege does not require intentionally seeking gain.

Privilege does not brush away the value of hard work. Many people rightfully pride themselves on their individual efforts; however, as this book will explore, members of nonprivileged groups are more likely to face barriers to educational and economic opportunities. Moreover, members of dominant groups enjoy the benefit of the doubt that their position is due to initiative alone. A White male who gets an executive position is less likely to be suspected of being a *token* hire than is a woman of color. For more thorough analysis, readers may consult Adams, & Bell (2016), McIntosh (1988), and Swalwell (2013).

If you're in a dominant group, maybe you're thinking, "What privilege? I know a person from a [nondominant group] who has it better than me." This brings us to *intersectionality,* the idea that we have multiple, overlapping identities that can grant advantages in one category and disadvantages in another (Crenshaw, 1991). For example, a former student, a White female who grew up in poverty, initially resisted the idea of White privilege. But when students of color from the same socioeconomic situation shared the discrimination they faced when seeking a job and applying for a loan, the White student realized that her race got her in the door more easily. The point is not to keep score in a contest of oppression, but rather to recognize that our complex identities reflect interconnected hierarchies.

To counter oppression, social justice aims to dismantle unjust systems and structures. Social justice aims for an outcome—"full and equitable participation" by members of all social groups (Bell, 2016, p. 1)—through an inclusive process that's "mutually shaped" to meet everyone's needs. From this perspective, society is not a fixed hierarchy, but rather a circle that can grow larger and provide opportunities to all (Clegg, 1989).

Discussion or Reflection

- How would you describe the relationship between sustainability and social justice?
- Return to your definition of sustainability. To what extent is social justice already embedded?
- How would you adapt your definition, if at all?

This book takes the stance that sustainability and social justice are inseparable, and that references to one include the other. Nonetheless, at times we may foreground the term *sustainability* or *social justice* in the context of commonly associated concepts (e.g., the environment and sustainability; discrimination and social justice).

With our big definitions under our belts, let's continue the thread by defining *educating for sustainability and social justice* in the introduction to Part II, coming right up.

References

Agyeman, J., Bullard, R. D., & Evans, B. (Eds.). (2003). *Just sustainabilities: Development in an unequal world*. Cambridge, MA: MIT Press.

Bell, L. A. (2016). Theoretical foundations for social justice education. In M. Adams & L. A. Bell (Eds.), *Teaching for diversity and social justice* (3rd ed., pp. 3–26). Abingdon, UK: Routledge.

Clegg, S. R. (1989). *Frameworks of power*. London, UK: Sage.

Crenshaw, K. (1991). Mapping the margins: Intersectionality, identity politics, and violence against women of color. *Stanford Law Review, 43*(6), 1241–1299.

Daly, H. E. (1996). Sustainable growth? No thank you. In J. Mander (Ed.), *The case against the global economy: And for a turn toward the local* (pp. 192–196). Abingdon, UK: Routledge.

Delgado, R. (1989). Symposium: Legal storytelling. *Michigan Law Review, 87*(2073), 223–236.

Feinstein, N. (2009). Education for sustainable development in the United States of America. In J. Laessøe, K. Schnack, S. Breiting, & S. Rolls (Eds.), *Climate change and sustainable development: The response from education* (pp. 309–355). Copenhagen, Denmark: Danish School of Education, University of Aarhus.

Jickling, B. (2001). Environmental thought, the language of sustainability, and digital watches. *Environmental Education Research, 7*(2), 167–180.

Ladson-Billings, G. (1998). Just what is critical race theory and what's it doing in a nice field like education? *International Journal of Qualitative Studies in Education, 11*(1), 7–24.

McIntosh, P. (1988). *White privilege: Unpacking the invisible knapsack*. Philadelphia, PA: Women's International League for Peace and Freedom.

Sneddon, C., Howarth, R. B., & Norgaard, R. B. (2006). Sustainable development in a post-Brundtland world. *Ecological Economics, 57*(2), 253–268.

Stephan, W. (1999). *Reducing prejudice and stereotyping in schools*. New York, NY: Teachers College Press.

Swalwell, K. M. (2013). *Educating activist allies: Social justice pedagogy with the suburban and urban elite*. Abingdon, UK: Routledge.

World Commission on Environment and Development. (1987). *Report of the World Commission on Environment and Development: Our common future*. New York, NY: WCED.

PART II

What's at Stake in Our Curriculum?

If sustainability means that communities can thrive into the future within the means of the environment, then what is education for sustainability? Education for sustainable development[1] (ESD) is the process of developing citizens who fulfill this vision. That's the short answer. But as a many-layered concept, educating for sustainability is best defined by its principles rather than by a single sentence.

Like sustainability itself, ESD rests on a set of values and principles that include ecological integrity, equity, ethics, and interdependence. There are other parallels as well: Just as sustainability positions the economy within the environment, ESD nests schools within communities. Just as social justice is embedded in sustainability, educational equity is central to ESD. And, just as the Sustainable Development Goals measure progress in more than dollars, achievement in ESD means much more than test scores. The goal is living well with others on a shared planet, and progress is judged by the strength of our communities and the level of opportunity afforded to all. ESD thus prepares citizens to play multiple roles:

- A systems thinker who integrates ecological, economic, and equity literacies;
- A critical thinker who makes ethical decisions;
- An effective problem-solver with an eye toward the public good;
- A peacemaker;
- An empathetic family member, neighbor, coworker, and citizen; and
- A physically and emotionally healthy individual.

In terms of school governance and its economic implications, ESD and social justice uphold education as a public good with a public purpose. The "Commons" of learning is treated as an open and abundant resource, not an enclosed commodity made scarce through market forces. Businesses and philanthropists are also stake-holders, but they do not dictate curriculum, funding, or accountability. Instead, schools are accountable to the community.

ESD is not without its detractors. For example, echoing the criticism aimed at sustainable development itself—that it prioritizes business-as-usual economic growth and sidelines social equity and the environment—detractors of ESD argue that it perpetuates the same faulty assumptions, diverting attention from the true roots of our ecological crisis: anthropocentric thinking (Kopnina, 2014). In response, this book tackles anthropocentrism from multiple angles.

Educating for Social Justice

Like ESD, educating for social justice (ESJ) is a learning process that aims for its eponymous outcome (Bell, 2016). ESJ draws from a family of pedago-gies, including democratic education, critical pedagogy, and culturally respon-sive teaching (CRT)—philosophical foundations we'll examine in Chapter 4 (Dover, 2013). ESJ overlaps in many ways with that of ESD: Both are partici-patory, grounded in students' lives, and support students to envision and bring about a more equitable future (Santone, 2003).

Like ESD, ESJ is contested. For example, Hansen (2001) and Campbell (2008a) suggested that ESJ steps beyond the teacher's ethical mandate for moral behaviors and accountability within the classroom. Pointing to the politically charged discourse of social justice, Campbell (2008b) contended, "Teachers should be moral agents and moral models, not moralistic activists" (p. 612). True, a commitment to social justice does not mean teachers should turn the classroom into a bully pulpit for political activism where students are treated "as a means to an end" (Hansen, 2001, p. 188). However, the following chapters will argue that the scale of inequalities makes *teaching for change* ethical and necessary.

ESD and ESJ come together with this bottom line: Both aim for educational solutions that support the development of the whole child, address institutional inequalities, ensure a healthy environment, and maintain public access to and control of schooling.

These broad strokes show that reorienting education toward ESD and so-cial justice is not about an Earth Day lesson here or a multicultural celebration there. Rather, these movements require a transformation of why, what, and how we teach. ESD and ESJ not only infuse meaning into curriculum but also reframe the very purpose of education. Therefore, the real question of Part II is *What's the story we want for education?*

We'll answer this question in the next three chapters as follows:

- Chapter 4 outlines the philosophies, pedagogies, and competencies needed to teach for sustainability and social justice, regardless of grade or discipline.

- Chapter 5 exposes detrimental practices and mindsets that undermine ESD and ESJ.
- Chapter 6 picks up the ideas in Chapter 4 and introduces more specific student outcomes and teaching strategies. Ample tables and frameworks (some on the book's website) show alignment across grades and disciplines.

The Part II Culminating Activities compile the best practices into rubrics (also on the book's website) that you'll use to evaluate a unit or course to reframe using the steps in Part III.

A closing thought: Curren (2009) asserted that ESD is both "compatible with" and "essential to sound education" (p. 38). This is a bold statement—one Part II sets out to prove.

Note

1 ESD is the terminology used globally. In the United States, educating for sustainability (EfS) is also used.

References

Bell, L. A. (2016). Theoretical foundations of social justice education. In M. Adams & L.A. Bell (Eds.), *Teaching for diversity and social justice* (3rd ed., pp. 3–26). New York, NY: Routledge.

Campbell, E. (2008a). The ethics of teaching as a moral profession. *Curriculum Inquiry, 38*(4), 357–385.

Campbell, E. (2008b). Teaching ethically as a moral condition of professionalism. In L. Nucci & D. Narvaez (Eds.), *Handbook of moral and character education* (pp. 601–617). New York, NY: Routledge.

Curren, R. (2009). Education for sustainable development: A philosophical assessment. *Impact, 2009*(18), 1–68.

Dover, A. G. (2013). Teaching for social justice: From conceptual frameworks to classroom practices. *Multicultural Perspectives, 15*(1), 3–11.

Hansen, D. T. (2001). *Exploring the moral heart of teaching: Toward a teacher's creed.* New York, NY: Teachers College Press.

Kopnina, H. (2014). Revisiting education for sustainable development (ESD): Examining anthropocentric bias through the transition of environmental education to ESD. *Sustainable Development, 22*(2), 73–83.

Santone, S. (2003). Education for sustainability. *Educational Leadership, 61*(4), 60–63.

4

WHAT'S THE STORY WE WANT FOR OUR TEACHING?

The convergence of social and ecological crises forces us to ask, "What does the world need from students—and what do they need from us?" The demands are daunting. We must create a classroom where all students are understood and valued; engage them in authentic, culturally relevant ways; design curriculum to foster democracy, community, and sustainability; and demonstrate an unwavering commitment to equity (Banks & Banks, 2001). Moreover, we must persevere at this as our professional responsibility to advocate for children, families, and communities.

These are what it means to be a "sustainability literate" educator: one with "the ability and disposition to engage in thinking, problem-solving, decision-making, and actions associated with achieving sustainability" (Nolet, 2009, p. 421). But K–12 teachers are already held to a comprehensive set of professional standards, and understandably you may be thinking, "Great. More work." This chapter will allay your concerns, framed by the following questions:

1. How do current professional education standards align with the competencies needed to teach for sustainability and social justice?
2. What related philosophies and pedagogies provide the foundation for reframing the curriculum?

To provide answers, the chapter introduces a set of competencies that define *teacher effectiveness* based on mainstream requirements and those needed to teach for sustainability and social justice. Next, the chapter introduces a set of pedagogical principles to guide curriculum design, regardless of grade or discipline. Looking ahead, Chapter 6 drills deeper into more age- and discipline-specific student outcomes and teaching strategies. The tools and frameworks there will equip you for course- or unit-level changes in your content area in Part III. Of course, getting to this—the story we want for our curriculum—will require slaying some dragons, and that's what you'll do in Chapter 5: Tackle the educational practices and mindsets that create and replicate the Story of More.

Let's get started.

How Do Current Professional Education Standards Align With the Competencies Needed To Teach for Sustainability and Social Justice?

Professional standards for K–12 educators are prescribed by the Interstate Teacher Assessment and Support Consortium (InTASC), a consortium of state education agencies responsible for licensing teacher education programs. Created in 1987 by the Chief Council of State School Officers (CCSSO), InTASC's 2013 Model Core Teaching Standards (MCTS) address four core areas (CCSSO, 2013): The Learner and Learning, Content Knowledge, Instructional Practice, and Professional Responsibility. This "common core" of standards (p. 3, *quotes in original*) is applicable to all educators and "define and support ongoing teacher effectiveness to ensure students reach college and career ready standards" (CCSSO, 2013).

At first glance, the language appears to reinforce the same old paradigm of standards-based accountability; the nod to "college and career readiness" is straight from Common Core State Standards, also developed by the CCSSO (2013). But read further and you'll find a larger purpose: to prepare educators for

> a transformed public education system—one that empowers every learner to take ownership of their learning, that emphasizes the … application of knowledge and skill to real world problems, [and] that values the differences each learner brings to the learning experience.
>
> (*CCSSO, 2013, p. 3*)

These ambitious targets are echoed throughout the standards. For example, the Content and Instructional Practices categories call for the use of "differing perspectives to engage learners in critical thinking, creativity, and collaborative problem solving related to authentic local and global issues" (CCSSO, 2013, p. 28). Teachers must also understand the influence of cultural differences to create "inclusive learning environments" (CCSSO, 2013, p. 8), build relationships with families and communities, and help learners develop in multiple realms (e.g., cognitively and linguistically).

Clearly the MCTS align closely with key principles of sustainability and social justice; however, neither term appears in the 57-page MCTS document

(CCSSO, 2013). Does this mean we must squeeze yet more content into an already crowded teacher preparation curriculum? Thankfully, no, as Nolet (2009) assured us that sustainability and social justice "provide strategies for addressing the challenges teacher education faces today" (p. 57). That said, we must be intentional with our implementation of MCTS in order to successfully develop sustainability-literate teachers and students. Otherwise, teacher education may simply reproduce the practices now contributing to unsustainability (Greenwood, 2010).

What Philosophies and Pedagogies Provide the Foundation?

Let's begin with a few definitions.[1] By *philosophy*, we refer to sets of beliefs and worldviews about the purpose of education (i.e., *why* and *what for*; Provenzo, Renaud, & Provenzo, 2009). A related term, *theory*, is an explanation of why or how something occurs. The words *methodology*, *pedagogy*, and *practice* refer to the applications of philosophies. Given the difficulty of talking about one term without the others, we'll also use the generic term "approach."

Recall from Part I that sustainability is often framed with three core dimensions: the environment, the economy, and equity (i.e., social justice). Here, we will add more nuance with the addition of *social action* (to emphasize real-world applications) and *well-being* (because that's the ultimate goal). To ensure curriculum speaks to these dimensions, let's introduce four pedagogical guidelines to frame the rest of this chapter (the order of presentation does not reflect their relative importance):

1. Embed the environmental dimension through environmental education (EE) and place-based education (PBE).
2. Support equity and social action through democratic education, critical pedagogy, and ecojustice education (which also integrates the environmental dimension).
3. Strengthen equity and inclusion through culturally responsive teaching (CRT).
4. Promote well-being by supporting physical- and social-emotional health.

The economic dimension of sustainability (introduced in Chapters 1–3) will be covered in greater depth in Chapters 5 and 6.

Given the breadth of sustainability and social justice, you might consider the pedagogies in the preceding guidelines as "subfields" (McKeown & United States Teacher Education for Sustainable Development Network, 2013, p. 36). And while you'll find new terminology, you'll discover that the guidelines are not only related and complementary, but also consistent with what you already know about engaging students and building relationships—meaning the approaches are "just good teaching" (Ladson-Billings, 1995a, p. 159).

Guideline 1. Embed the Environmental Dimension Through Environmental and Place-Based Education

Throughout the book we've emphasized that human-created institutions (including educational systems) are embedded within ecological ones. This makes ecological and environmental literacy a cornerstone of ESD. While there's been scholarly debate about exact definitions, we'll frame ecological literacy as knowledge of the life science aspects of the environment (e.g., ecosystems, flows of energy) and environmental literacy as a broader concept that includes (a) the ability to "analyze global, social, cultural, political, economic and environmental relationships"; and (b) the skills needed to make "responsible decisions as individuals, as members of their communities, and as citizens of the world" (McBride, Brewer, Berkowitz, & Borrie, 2013; North American Association for Environmental Education, 1999, p. 2).

As a related field, place-based education situates environmental literacy in the local places students inhabit. In PBE, the community is the starting point for investigations that use "all aspects of the local environment, including local cultural and historical information" to teach across disciplines (Sobel, 2004, p. 1). Learning activities can range from outdoor exploration to classroom-based lessons (Woodhouse & Knapp, 2000). PBE is not simply about, for example, studying local history as a point of interest. Rather, PBE cultivates students' identities as members of ecological and civic communities with the capacity to solve shared problems (DeFelice, Adams, Branco, & Pieroni, 2014). When used as the basis for project-based learning (an approach popular in many schools), PBE provides immediate relevance; students engage with issues right outside their doors and naturally raise questions complex enough to support meaningful projects.

For example, in a rural community in Oregon, students in an interdisciplinary STEM course focused on the redevelopment of a *brownfield* (a contaminated site) located on school property. Working with state and local agencies, students investigated the history of the site, soil and water quality, and associated health risks. As a final project, students created redevelopment proposals and presented them at a state brownfields conference. (The teacher won a 2016 national award from the U.S. Environmental Protection Agency.)

While PBE prioritizes local concerns, it can also be a gateway to parallel global topics (McKeown & Hopkins, 2005). For example, learning about local ecosystems would precede studying the rainforest. To bridge the two, students might compare the two ecosystems and (as age-appropriate) learn about indigenous tribes, the impacts of industrialization, revitalization movements, and ways our own consumption habits affect it all. Including these social justice dimensions can counter the critique that some approaches to EE and PBE neglect—or even reinforce—colonial mindsets by remaining silent on the cultural or ecological ramifications of development (Baldwin, 2009; Haymes, 1995; McLean, 2013).

The emphasis on engagement and equity in PBE and EE leads us to our next tenet.

Guideline 2. Support Equity and Social Action Through Democratic Education, Critical Pedagogy, and Ecojustice Education

As a long-standing cornerstone of democracy, public education should arguably provide opportunities for students to experience democracy in public life. But what does this mean?

When I ask educators what "democracy" brings to mind, common responses include voting (always #1), citizenship, government, following the law, and patriotism. These responses conceptualize democracy as a civic duty or a social studies topic, overlooking democracy as a set of social values: equality under the law, the pursuit of the common good, informed decision-making, and ethical participation in self-governance (Apple & Beane, 1995; Barber, 1989). From this perspective, democracy is both a noun and a verb—a goal reached through intentional action.

But this does not happen on its own. John Dewey (1859–1952), a grandfather of democratic education, asserted that democratic societies require an education that "gives individuals a personal interest in social relationships ... and the habits of mind which secure social change" (1916/2004, p. 95). In their role as young citizens, students learn to connect their own self-interest to that of society to effect change at both levels (Sleeter, 2012). Democratic education aligns learning to these ends (Giroux & McLaren, 1986), and thus overlaps with outcomes in the MCTS, including critical thinking, problem-solving, and global awareness.

Democratic educators also pursue social justice. They refuse to accept oppression as inevitable and accept the obligation to not only "lessen the harshness of social inequities in school," but also to "change the conditions that create them" (Apple & Beane, 1995, p. 11). Giroux and McLaren (1986) thus called upon educators to be "transformative intellectuals" (p. 215) who interrupt the racial and socioeconomic inequalities perpetuated by the educational process itself. (We'll explore this more in Chapter 5.)

The goal of social change is a point of intersection between democratic education and critical pedagogy, a philosophy focused on analyzing, critiquing, and ultimately changing oppressive structures to expand "freedom, justice, and happiness" (Bentz & Shapiro, 1998, p. 146). Critical theorists have asserted that injustice breeds not only in economic and educational systems, but also through the narrative that marginalized people deserve their position (Ladson-Billings, 1998)—a script that's especially destructive when it's internalized (Burbules & Berk, 1999).

But changing inequitable forces requires naming them. Brazilian educator Paulo Freire (1970/1986) called this *conscentizacao* (p. 19), a process of "reading the world" using one's own experiences as the "text" (Freire & Macedo, 2005). *Conscentizacao* arose from Freire's work among peasant communities colonized by the Portuguese. His seminal work, *Pedagogy of the Oppressed* (1970/1986), outlined the role of education in "decolonizing" place and identity through "the elimination of dehumanizing oppression" (p. 93). For Freire, education was an emancipatory process in which *conscentizacao* precedes formal education (Freire & Macedo, 2005).

The potential for transformation in the theories presented means that neutrality is no longer an option. This poses educators with an ethical choice: Will we perpetuate injustice through inaction or advocate for change?

If we choose advocacy, we must define our boundaries, as Liston and Zeichner (1987) advised. While agreeing that teachers need to take an ethical stance, the authors drew a line between incorporating democratic values into instruction and rallying students to "support a particular political cause" (p. 16). The former is needed to critically evaluate social conditions; the latter coerces children to agree with positions they may not accept or be too young to understand.

Consider a mock school election in a fifth-grade classroom. Supporting students to assess how candidates' positions align with, for example, the principle of equal rights is appropriate; telling students which candidate is "the right one" is not. This echoes the distinction set forth in the introduction to this book: Teachers must advocate for equity and the common good and develop students' capacity to make ethical decisions based on this. Simply proselytizing removes the educational component and turns students into a passive audience rather than active citizens. Moreover, as discussed in the Introduction to Part II, if we pontificate rather than educate, we abuse our authority and fuel critics who contend that social justice is beyond the scope of an educator's moral duties (Campbell, 2008). The key is to establish democratic ideals in the classroom and continuously use them as an ethical grounding for inquiry. In Chapter 6, we'll look at some discipline-specific ways to do this.

As noted, some forms of EE have been critiqued for their scant attention to social justice. On the flip side, critical pedagogy has drawn reproach for neglecting ecological concerns. The oversights on either side force an artificial divide between environmental and social concerns (Bowers, 2005; Gruenewald & Smith, 2014). In response is the field of ecojustice education, a "pedagogy of responsibility" that recognizes ecological degradation and social oppression as manifestations of the same problems: anthropocentrism and notions of progress based on industrialization (Martusewicz & Edmundson, 2005, p. 72). (Recall how these themes arose in Chapter 2, "The Story of More.")

Like critical pedagogy, ecojustice education recognizes the ethical obligations to confront social problems. However, ecojustice scholars warn that molding students into self-directed, transformational actors runs the risk of breaking bonds with the time-honored values and wisdom that contribute to sustainability, such as an orientation toward community, folk knowledge, or other traditions passed down through generations (Cajete, 1994). From this perspective, taken-for-granted mantras such as "think for yourself" privilege individual autonomy, implying that learning has no basis in community (Bowers, 2001; Martusewicz & Edmundson, 2005). This counters all we have said about interdependence and the ways "acting, being, and knowing" connect people and place (Stetsenko, 2008, p. 471). Ecojustice pedagogy thus asks, "What do we need to conserve?" as well as "What needs to be transformed?" (Martusewicz, Edmundson, & Lupinacci, 2011, p. 18). To answer this, ecojustice stresses the revitalization of community bonds, noncommodified exchanges, and biological and linguistic diversity (Bowers, 2005).

As further caution, ecojustice theorists uncover ways individualism is embedded in *orthodoxies* such as Maslow's hierarchy of needs, which positions self-actualization at the top (Bowers, 1995; Martusewicz et al., 2011). These points are well taken, as they unearth ways the Story of More's mindsets are etched into education in hidden ways. This raises further caveats about student autonomy and authority: When is it appropriate for students to think for themselves, and when is individualistic thinking a rejection of community or democratic values? The student who advocates for a racially pure ethnostate can easily play the "thinking for myself" card. Likewise, when it comes to decision-making, students' participation must be scaled to their developmental readiness. First graders are capable of weighing in on which books to read at storytime—not on the nuances of the district budget.

Applying this insight to our story metaphor for curriculum design, ecojustice education reveals the importance of age-appropriate plots as well as the need to balance narratives of individual heroes saving the day with stories of communities that solve problems together. The same goes for the role of the teacher. While we know the difference an effective teacher can make, hero tropes popularized in movies such as *Freedom Writers* peddle the idea that classroom learning alone is sufficient to compensate for the inequalities outside of school (Rothstein, 2008).

Discussion Questions

1. Can you identify any common threads among the approaches we've covered?
2. Do you use any of the teaching practices described, even if under different names (e.g., student-centered learning)?
3. What practices seem most related to your discipline? Which seem furthest away?

Guideline 3. Strengthen Equity and Inclusion Through CRT

As discussed, the MCTS calls for teachers to support learners of all backgrounds. This requires understanding our own cultural frames, how they influence our actions, and the impacts (intended or not) on the "fairness and equity" of the educational experience (National Governors Association Center for Best Practices [NGA] & CCSSO, 2013, p. 44). The demographic imbalance between the teaching force (which is about 80% non-Hispanic White) and the student body (now more than 50% students of color) elevates the importance of intercultural literacy in advancing equity (Taie & Goldring, 2017).

Sounds great. But what exactly do we mean by "culture"?

Culture refers to the collection of learned values, behaviors, attitudes, and practices shared by a group of people or an institution (Ember & Ember, 1988). Culture includes physical and material objects; language, stories, and music; behaviors, norms, and social rules; and attitudes, beliefs, and values. Through ongoing socialization, we acquire culture through interactions among individuals, families, institutions such as schools, and the communities they are nested in (Bronfenbrenner, 1977, 1986).

The terms *culture* and *diversity* are often used as references to people of color. But such usage is problematic because it presumes that whiteness is neutral and that diversity is something others possess in comparison. This obscures an important fact: Notions of "regular" and "different" are social constructs—a result of the dominant group's power to project its ways as normal and natural (Bell, Adams, & Griffin, 2007). Educators must bear in mind that diversity is about our collective differences, not degrees of variance or exoticness measured in relation to those assumed to be "unmarked" by race or ethnicity. A mixed race, low-income, transgender girl who uses a wheelchair is not more diverse than a White, middle-class, able-bodied heterosexual male (although the latter likely garners more advantages based on his social groups).

In terms of culture and pedagogy, a set of related theories appears in the literature under various names: *culturally relevant* (Ladson-Billings 1995b), *culturally responsive* (Gay, 2010), *culturally sustaining* (Paris, 2012), *multicultural education* (Banks & Banks, 2001; Dover, 2009, 2013); *reality pedagogy* (Emdin, 2016); and *critical hip hop pedagogy* (Akom, 2009). While the distinctions among these terms are important (see Dover, 2009), we will look at selected approaches, beginning with CRT.

Culturally Responsive Teaching

To clarify upfront, CRT is not necessarily about "covering" cultures in the curriculum (addressed in Chapter 6). Rather, the larger goal is connecting content in *any* discipline to students' cultural frames, experiences, and communities in order to "expand [students'] intellectual horizons and academic achievement" (Gay, 2002, p. 109).

One way to honor both culture and individuality is by building on students' "funds of knowledge": their experiences, talents, and prior learning as well as their language, families, and community values (Moll, Amanti, Neff, & Gonzalez, 1992). To do so, teachers must identify authentic connections that can form bridges to academic learning (Delpit, 2006). For example, students' family histories can provide entry points into geography and social studies content. Age-appropriate community data (e.g., census figures, public health information) provide real-world examples of math in our everyday lives. Like PBE, CRT reaches into the community, recognizing that "high status" academic knowledge is not the sole authoritative source of learning (Apple & Beane, 1995, p. 13).

Teachers should also be aware of the *currencies and capital* students depend on. Do you have students who share a car with another family, grow their own food, or barter (perhaps when money is not available)? Such practices help students navigate everyday life, and recognizing this enables us to see value in skills we might otherwise overlook, such as entrepreneurship or caretaking (Santone & Saunders, 2013). This broadens the definition of achievement and averts deficit narratives that see only what students seemingly lack, a topic addressed in Chapter 5.

We must be clear that there are no fixed ethnic learning styles. Culture certainly influences—but does not determine—the learning experience, and making generalizations denies students' individuality (Guild, 1994). Likewise, the theory of hardwired learning styles (e.g., auditory vs. visual) has been discredited as a "neuromyth" (Dekker, Lee, Howard-Jones, & Jolles, 2012; Newton, 2015). Narrowly teaching based on a specific learning style—whether attributed to culture or brain structure—assumes that learning modalities (e.g., visual or kinesthetic) are isolated, a falsehood that overlooks the significant "transfer of information" that occurs within the brain (Dekker et al., 2012, para. 2). While students may have learning preferences, it is important to use a range of teaching strategies—sound advice in any context (Tomlinson, 2014).

Critical Hip Hop Pedagogy

Cultural relevance meets critical pedagogy through Critical Hip Hop Pedagogy, an approach that engages youth (particularly African Americans) in social activism (Alim, 2011). Bruce and Davis (2000) defined *hip hop* as "urban-based creativity and expression of culture," and *rap* as "the style of rhythm-spoken words across a musical terrain" (p. 122). Scholars such as Akom (2009) saw the "liberatory potential" (p. 54) of these popular genres to call out problems such as racism and misogyny—although Akom acknowledged that some aspects of hip hop do "quite the opposite."

In terms of identity development, hip hop's themes of resistance and emancipation can counter narratives of inferiority before they take root (Bartolomé & Macedo, 1997). Moreover, hip hop's roots in African oral traditions provide rich content as well as a bridge to analyzing other forms of language (Hill, 2009). For example, students in a language arts class deconstructed hip hop music and lyrics to learn concepts such as beat, rhythm, and stanza, and then applied them to the study of Shakespeare (Delpit, 1995). Other educators have assigned students to rewrite derogatory lyrics as a way to turn the tables on harmful messages.

Recognizing the strong correlation between limited verbal facility and aggression (Kindlon and Thompson, 1999), educators have used hip hop poetry "slams" to help students name and understand their emotions through prompts such as, "I just don't get it when ... I get so angry when ..." (Bruce & Davis, 2000, p. 124; Gilligan, 1996). By equipping students to discover power through language instead of violence, hip hop poetry can cultivate skills in both literacy and conflict resolution (Cafazzo, 1999). Hip hop scholars again remind us that positive applications of hip hop empower students to oppose—not embrace—brutality, sexism, and negative identity development (Alim, 2011).

Regardless of our strategy to bring students' lives into teaching, the connection must be significant and authentic enough to open new horizons. As we'll examine in Chapter 5, some approaches to integrating culture actually shut down learning.

Code-Switching

While it is important to build upon students' linguistic knowledge, it is equally necessary to teach students the modes of communication expected in academic and career contexts. To be successful, students—and all of us—must adapt language and behaviors to different situations such as family, work, or leisure time. Think about it: Do you greet a small child and your supervisor the same way? Would you wear to work what you wear to the beach? These contextual shifts in language, dress, and body language are known as *code-switching* (Wheeler, 2008).

While we all code switch, there's an equity dimension because social narratives tell us that some ways of speaking are better than others. Society assigns value to different forms of expression and elevates some above others. The *right* language and behaviors are those typically required in academic and professional settings, which reflect the "discourse patterns, interactional styles, and spoken and written language" of the dominant group (Delpit, 1988, p. 285). Delpit used the term "culture of power" to describe these codes. The unquestioned correctness of these norms is so entrenched that they remain invisible to those who define them. But we must become aware. It's our job to help students fulfill their potential, and that includes teaching students to use the *power* norms when the situation demands it.

Maybe you're thinking, "Wait. Aren't we supposed to validate students' languages?" Yes. But teachers also have an obligation to help students expand their linguistic repertoire and select the right cultural *tools* for each situation. To deny this to students—even in the service of relevance—is to deny them opportunities.

Language arts is one obvious discipline to embed code-switching. Wheeler (2008) described a teacher who helps young students compare the grammatical patterns of their home language with those of formal language (e.g., "he be" vs. "he is"), recognizing that both are legitimate. But code-switching has a place in other disciplines as well. For example, to investigate local public safety concerns, middle school students interviewed residents about their experiences. For this, students captured data through forms of communication used within the community, such as social media posts from the neighborhood watch group. Students supplemented this with high status data from the census and law enforcement agencies. After compiling the information into a range of formats (formal reports and presentations, collections of personal stories), students presented their work to local leaders at a public forum. To prepare, students rehearsed professional greetings, including eye contact and handshakes. Such strategies simultaneously meet the goals of democratic education and PBE, critical pedagogy, and culturally relevant teaching. Code-switching is also a way to meet Common Core Speaking and Listening Standards, which require "flexible communication" and the ability to "adapt speech to context and task" (NGA & CCSSO, 2010).

In short, code-switching is applicable any time a discipline or topic requires students to make informed choices about language and behavior. But to do this in a way that supports equity, educators must always keep two points in mind. First, compared with students in the dominant culture, those in nondominant groups bear a heavier burden of adaptation to shake off the stigmas imposed by the dominant culture; being accepted requires vigilant compliance with privileged norms that are resistant to (or even exempt from) having to bend in the other direction. Second, cultural hierarchies are socially constructed, and students' ways of being are not inherently defective—perceptions deem them so (Alim, 2011). This recognition enables us to see students' cultural capital as an asset as opposed to a deficit. (In that deficit mindset, we teach students the power codes, but only because we've decided their own languages are inferior.)

Guideline 4. Promote Well-Being by Supporting Physical and Social-Emotional Health

In Chapter 1, we introduced a conception of well-being that integrates physical and mental health. In this section, we'll examine three ways to support this: free play, exposure to nature, and social-emotional learning (SEL). (In Chapter 6 we'll look at trauma-informed practice, an area related to SEL.) Of course, food and nutrition are vital for wellness, but given this book focuses on curriculum, we won't address school food programs here.

Free Play and Exposure to Nature

"All work and no play makes Johnny a dull boy," the adage goes. But a dearth of play can also make him obese, anxious, and depressed.

The proverbial advice has never been more relevant for today's tech-saturated youth. Children ages 8 and older spend up to 9 hours a day in front of electronic devices, from computers to phones (Common Sense Media, 2015). Screen time for young children now exceeds the recommendations of the American Association of Pediatrics: little to no exposure for children younger than 18 months, and a 1-hour limit up to age 5 (Hill et al., 2016). Regardless of age, excessive media consumption eats into time for playing, exercising, and interacting with family and friends. Together, this can contribute to sadness, boredom, and lower academic achievement (Rideout, Foehr, & Roberts, 2010).

Free, outdoor play—especially exploring nature—can be a powerful remedy; decades of research show the positive effects of physical activity and exposure to nature on students' academic achievement and mental health (Bell et al., 2008; Lester & Maudsley, 2006; Pellegrini & Davis, 1993). However, youth today spend far less time outdoors—especially in natural settings—than their parents' generation did (Pergams, & Zaradic, 2008). Richard Louv's 2005 best seller *Last Child in the Woods* brought the problem of "nature deficit disorder" to the public's attention. The book set off alarm bells, mobilizing educators and parents to advocate for free play and outdoor learning—just when high-stakes testing under No Child Left Behind was calling the shots. Did schools take heed? Find out in Chapter 5.

Outdoor exploration also correlates with proenvironment behavior. Numerous studies show that children's emotional connections to nature—not simply environmental knowledge—is the strongest predictor of stewardship behavior as an adult (Kollmuss & Agyeman, 2002; Wells & Lekies, 2006). Here, we see how EE, PBE, and student wellness all come together.

Social and Emotional Learning

Another important aspect of student health falls under the umbrella of SEL. The Collaborative for Academic, Social, and Emotional Learning (CASEL, 2017), SEL's flagship organization since 1994, offers this definition:

> SEL is the process through which children and adults acquire and effectively apply the knowledge, attitudes, and skills necessary to understand and manage emotions, set and achieve positive goals, feel and show empathy for others, establish and maintain positive relationships, and make responsible decisions.
>
> *(para. 1)*

CASEL's (2017) framework for SEL identifies five core competencies: self-awareness, self-management, social awareness, relationship skills, and responsible decision-making. Within these realms are more specific skills such as recognizing one's emotions, understanding other people's perspectives, self-regulation, and the ability to forge healthy relationships.

A growing body of evidence shows that SEL competencies can help students manage individual behaviors, improve personal relationships, and support academic success in and beyond school. For example, analyses indicate that investments in SEL in early childhood education can save society future costs on remedial education, crime, substance abuse, and public assistance (Dodge et al., 2015; Jones, Karoly, Crowley, & Greenberg, 2015; Washington State Institute for Public Policy, 2017). SEL is also linked to higher academic achievement, which in turn leads to better job prospects and higher incomes (Heckman, Pinto, & Savelyev, 2013). While financial benefits should not be the sole or even primary measure of SEL's value, these numbers demonstrate yet again the inextricable link between individual and social well-being.

Likewise, physical, mental, academic, and social-emotional well-being go together. To maximize benefits, schools must make health and wellness just as important as academics, recognizing that they are all connected. One small step is embedded in the Every Student Succeeds Act (ESSA), which requires states to define a nonacademic indicator of school quality or student success, such as chronic absenteeism, discipline data, or even physical education. CASEL is now guiding states to integrate SEL into their implementation plans (Gayl, 2017). However, evidence-based measures of SEL are still evolving, making it premature to include them in teacher and school assessments (Blad, 2017). As we'll see in Chapter 5, this leaves SEL vulnerable to accusations that it is just a touchy-feely fad.

Strategies for integrating SEL can be both schoolwide (e.g., ensuring adequate time for recess, forming a cooking club) and classroom-based (e.g., outdoor exploration, building movement into activities).

Chapter Takeaways

We've looked at a constellation of pedagogies—some that emphasize the environment, others that focus on social change, and some that aim to reconcile both. Let's review some of the key understandings. (You'll encounter these ideas again as you proceed through the book.)

- Environmental/place-based education: Ground inquiry in the local environment, history, and culture. Cultivate a sense of belonging to ecological and cultural communities. Connect local actions and global impacts.
- Democratic education/critical pedagogy: Promote student voice and agency to bring about democratic ideals of justice and equity, in and out of the classroom. Uphold education as a public good.
- Ecojustice: Ecological degradation and cultural oppression stem from anthropocentrism and commodification of the Commons. Education must maintain and revitalize traditional knowledge and values about how to live sustainably.

- Culturally responsive teaching: Establish authentic relevance to students' lives, cultures, and communities. Recognize the socially constructed notions of *correct* language and behavior. Teachers must thus legitimize students' modes of communication, teach the codes of power, and help students discern when and how to use each.
- Wellness: Physical and social-emotional wellness support each other. Exposure to nature and free play can improve overall health.

Discussion Questions

1. Which of the takeaways are most significant for your practice? Are there other ideas you would add?
2. Can you give examples of how the key principles of one approach overlap with those of others?

Activity 4.1: Curriculum Mini-Makeovers

In this activity, you will review one- to two-sentence synopses of curriculum units (see Table 4.1) and suggest adaptations to better align them with the ideas presented in this chapter, resulting in a mini-makeover. To spur your thinking, consider questions such as *How could the unit engage students in a real-world issue? What changes could make the unit more culturally relevant? How could I integrate ideas of wellness?*

For example, consider a *before* unit in which high school students in a technology course use design software to plan their dream home. Students' plans include indoor pools, game rooms, and movie theaters. It's certainly a fun activity and the students enjoy it. But as is, the project fails to engage students in critical thinking about the environmental and socioeconomic aspects of housing, especially in their own communities. To adapt this unit in a mini-makeover, students could assess features of their own housing, examine housing in different parts of the world, evaluate the health effects and energy efficiency of different building materials, and uncover how family patterns (i.e., nuclear family vs. extended family) influence the concept of a desirable home. With a critical pedagogy lens, students might then look at affordability in their own communities (even for their own families). As a culminating project, students might design affordable *low footprint* housing units or work with the local housing authority on energy efficiency projects (e.g., insulation).

In an ideal world, the unit could do this and more. But we know that's not always possible in the face of mandates and standards. Not every unit or course can do it all, and nor is instruction inadequate if it emphasizes one pedagogy or philosophy over another. Right now, we're simply generating ideas for incremental changes as a step toward the more extensive reframing you'll do later in the book. (Note: As you create your adaptations, be ready to explain the changes you made and the specific pedagogies you drew upon).

TABLE 4.1 Curriculum Mini-Makeovers

Before	After
For kindergarten Diversity Day, children who have recently emigrated from Central America are the only ones asked to bring in special foods and wear costumes.	
As a culminating project in their Wild Animals unit, fourth graders in a community located near a national park select five animals from around the world they would most like to see in a "personal zoo."	
After a swastika and racially derogatory language is found spray-painted on lockers, a middle school history teacher decides not to discuss the incident in class in order to "remain neutral."	
In a low-income community with high levels of asthma and diabetes, a college physiology instructor at the local university provides textbook coverage of the major systems of the body with an emphasis on identification and memorization.	

This chapter has introduced the broad strokes of grounding curriculum in sustainability and social justice. We've seen strategies to center learning in the community, establish inclusive environments, and build healthy relationships with ourselves and the world around us. Teaching in this way is not a one-time thought exercise, but an ongoing professional obligation to be a reflective practitioners who "continually evaluate[s] ... the effects of his/her choices and actions on others," including "learners, families, other professionals, and the community" (CCSSO, 2013, Standard 9; Zeichner & Liston, 2013).

If these practices represent the story we want for our curriculum, what practices have hidden pitfalls that can trap us into replicating the story we don't want? That is the focus of Chapter 5.

Note

1 See Nolet (2009) for a more detailed analysis of these terms.

References

Akom, A. A. (2009). Critical hip hop pedagogy as a form of liberatory praxis. *Equity & Excellence in Education, 42*(1), 52–66.

Alim, H. S. (2011). Global ill-literacies: Hip hop cultures, youth identities, and the politics of literacy. *Review of Research in Education, 35*(1), 120–146.

Apple, M. W., & Beane, J. A. (1995). *Democratic schools.* Alexandria, VA: Association for Supervision and Curriculum Development.

Baldwin, A. (2009). Ethnoscaping Canada's boreal forest: Liberal whiteness and its disaffiliation from colonial space. *The Canadian Geographer/Le Géographe Canadien, 53*(4), 427–443.

Banks J. A., & Banks C. A. M. (Eds.). (2001). *Multicultural education: Issues and perspectives* (4th ed.). New York, NY: Wiley.

Barber, B. R. (1989). Public talk and civic action: Education for participation in a strong democracy. *Social Education, 53*(6), 355–356, 370.

Bartolomé, L., & Macedo, D. (1997). Dancing with bigotry: The poisoning of racial and ethnic identities. *Harvard Educational Review, 67*(2), 222–247.

Bell, L. A., Adams, M., & Griffin, P. (2007). *Teaching for diversity and social justice* (2nd ed.). New York, NY: Routledge.

Bell, S., Hamilton, V., Montarzino, A., Rothnic, H., Travlou, P., & Alves, S. (2008). *Greenspace and quality of life: A critical literature review.* Stirling, UK: Greenspace Scotland. Retrieved from http://www.greenspacescotland.org.uk/greenspace-and-quality-of-life.aspx

Bentz, V. M., & Shapiro, J. J. (1998). *Mindful inquiry in social research.* Thousand Oaks, CA: Sage.

Blad, E. (2017, August 10). Building a modern marshmallow test: New ways to measure social–emotional learning. *Education Week.* Retrieved from http://blogs.edweek. org/edweek/rulesforengagement/2017/08/building_a_modern_marshmallow_ test_new_ways_to_measure_social-emotional_learning.html

Bowers, C. A. (1995). *Educating for an ecologically sustainable culture: Rethinking moral education, creativity, intelligence, and other modern orthodoxies.* Albany, NY: State University of New York Press.

Bowers, C. A. (2001). *Educating for eco-justice and community.* Athens, Greece: University of Georgia Press.

Bowers, C. A. (2005). *The false promises of constructivist theories of learning: A global and ecological critique.* New York, NY: Peter Lang.

Bronfenbrenner, U. (1977). Toward an experimental ecology of human development. *American Psychologist, 32*(7), 513–531.

Bronfenbrenner, U. (1986). Ecology of the family as a context for human development: Research perspectives. *Developmental Psychology, 22*(6), 723–742.

Bruce, H. E., & Davis, B. D. (2000). Slam: Hip-hop meets poetry—a strategy for violence intervention. *The English Journal, 89*(5), 119–127.

Burbules, N. C., & Berk, R. (1999). Critical thinking and critical pedagogy: Relations, differences, and limits. In T. S. Popkewitz & L. Fendler (Eds.), *Critical theories in education: Changing terrains of knowledge and politics* (pp. 45–65). New York, NY: Routledge.

Cafazzo, D. (1999, July 24). Poetic lesson in nonviolence. *Tacoma News Tribune,* pp. A1.

Cajete, G. (1994). *Look to the mountain: An ecology of indigenous education.* Durango, CO: Kivaki Press.

Campbell, E. (2008). The ethics of teaching as a moral profession. *Curriculum Inquiry, 38*(4), 357–385.

Common Sense Media. (2015). *The common sense census: Media use by tweens and teens.* Retrieved from https://www.commonsensemedia.org/research/the-common-sense-census-media-use-by-tweens-and-teens

Council of Chief State School Officers. (2013, April). *InTASC model core teaching standards and learning progressions for teachers 1.0: A resource for ongoing teacher development.* Washington, DC: Author.

DeFelice, A., Adams, J. D., Branco, B., & Pieroni, P. (2014). Engaging underrepresented high school students in an urban environmental and geoscience place-based curriculum. *Journal of Geoscience Education, 62*(1), 49–60.

Dekker, S., Lee, N. C., Howard-Jones, P., & Jolles, J. (2012). Neuromyths in education: Prevalence and predictors of misconceptions among teachers. *Frontiers in Psychology, 3*, 1–8.

Delpit, L. (1988). The silenced dialogue: Power and pedagogy in educating other people's children. *Harvard Educational Review, 58*(3), 280–299.

Delpit, L. (1995). *Other people's children: Cultural conflict in the classroom.* New York, NY: The New Press.

Delpit, L. (2006). *Other people's children: Cultural conflict in the classroom* (2nd ed.). New York, NY: The New Press.

Dodge, K. A., Bierman, K. L., Coie, J. D., Greenberg, M. T., Lochman, J. E., McMahon, R. J., ... Pinderhughes, E. E. (2015). Impact of early intervention on psychopathology, crime, and well-being at age 25. *American Journal of Psychiatry, 172*(1), 59–70.

Dover, A. G. (2009). Teaching for social justice and K–12 student outcomes: A conceptual framework and research review. *Equity & Excellence in Education, 42*(4), 506–524.

Dover, A. G. (2013). Teaching for social justice: From conceptual frameworks to classroom practices. *Multicultural Perspectives, 15*(1), 3–11.

Ember, C., & Ember, M. (1988). *Anthropology* (5th ed.). Englewood Cliffs, NJ: Prentice Hall.

Emdin, C. (2016). *For White folks who teach in the hood ... and the rest of y'all too: Reality pedagogy and urban education.* Boston, MA: Beacon Press.

Freire, P. (1986). *Pedagogy of the oppressed* (M. B. Ramos, Trans.). New York, NY: Continuum. (Original work published 1970)

Freire, P., & Macedo, D. (2005). *Literacy: Reading the word and the world.* New York, NY: Routledge.

Gay, G. (2002). Preparing for culturally responsive teaching. *Journal of Teacher Education, 53*(2), 106–116.

Gay, G. (2010). *Culturally responsive teaching: Theory, research, and practice* (2nd ed.). New York, NY: Teachers College Press.

Gayl, C. L. (2017). *How state planning for the Every Student Succeeds Act (ESSA) can promote student academic, social, and emotional learning: An examination of five key strategies.* Chicago, IL: Collaborative for Academic, Social, and Emotional Learning. Retrieved from http://www.casel.org/wp-content/uploads/2017/04/ESSA-and-SEL-Five-Strategies-April-2017-041717.pdf

Gilligan, J. (1996). *Violence: Reflections on a national epidemic.* New York, NY: Vintage.

Giroux, H., & McLaren, P. (1986). Teacher education and the politics of engagement: The case for democratic schooling. *Harvard Educational Review, 56*(3), 213–239.

Greenwood, D. (2010, Fall). A critical analysis of sustainability education in schooling's bureaucracy: Barriers and small openings in teacher education. *Teacher Education Quarterly, 37*(4), 139–154.

Gruenewald, D. A., & Smith, G. A. (Eds.). (2014). *Place-based education in the global age: Local diversity.* New York, NY: Routledge.

Guild, P. (1994). The culture/learning style connection. *Educational Leadership, 51*(8), 16–21.

Haymes, S. N. (1995). *Race, culture, and the city: A pedagogy for Black urban struggle.* Albany, NY: State University of New York Press.

Heckman, J., Pinto, R., & Savelyev, P. (2013). Understanding the mechanisms through which an influential early childhood program boosted adult outcomes. *American Economic Review, 103*(6), 2052–2086.

Hill, D., Ameenuddin, N., Chassiakos, Y. L. R., Cross, C., Hutchinson, J., Levine, A., ... Swanson, W. S. (2016). Media and young minds. *Pediatrics, 138*(5), e20162591.

Hill, M. L. (2009). *Beats, rhymes, and classroom life: Hip-hop pedagogy and the politics of identity.* New York, NY: Teachers College Press.

Jones, D. E., Karoly, L. A., Crowley, D. M., & Greenberg, M. T. (2015). Considering valuation of noncognitive skills in benefit–cost analysis of programs for children. *Journal of Benefit–Cost Analysis, 6*(3), 471–507.

Kindlon, D., & Thompson, M. (1999). *Raising cain: Protecting the emotional life of boys.* New York, NY: Ballantine Books.

Kollmuss, A., & Agyeman, J. (2002). Mind the gap: Why do people act environmentally and what are the barriers to pro-environmental behavior? *Environmental Education Research, 8*(3), 239–260.

Ladson-Billings, G. (1995a). But that's just good teaching! The case for culturally relevant pedagogy. *Theory Into Practice, 34*(3), 159–165.

Ladson-Billings, G. (1995b). Toward a theory of culturally relevant pedagogy. *American Educational Research Journal, 32*(3), 465–491. doi:10.3102/00028312032003465

Ladson-Billings, G. (1998). Just what is critical race theory and what's it doing in a nice field like education? *International Journal of Qualitative Studies in Education, 11*(1), 7–24.

Lester, S., & Maudsley, M. (2006). *Play, naturally: A review of children's natural play.* London, England: Children's Play Council, National Children's Bureau. Retrieved from http://www.playday.org.uk/PDF/play-naturally-a-review-of-childrens-natural%20play.pdf

Liston, D. P., & Zeichner, K. M. (1987). Critical pedagogy and teacher education. *Journal of Education, 169*(3), 117–137.

Louv, R. (2005). *Last child in the woods: Saving our kids from nature-deficit disorder.* Chapel Hill, NC: Algonquin Books.

Martusewicz, R., & Edmundson, J. (2005). Social foundations as pedagogies of responsibility and eco-ethical commitment. In D. W. Butin (Ed.), *Teaching social foundations of education: Contexts, theories, and issues* (pp. 71–92). New York, NY: Routledge.

Martusewicz, R. A., Edmundson, J., & Lupinacci, J. (2011). *Ecojustice education: Toward diverse, democratic, and sustainable communities.* New York, NY: Routledge.

McBride, B. B., Brewer, C. A., Berkowitz, A. R., & Borrie, W. T. (2013). Environmental literacy, ecological literacy, ecoliteracy: What do we mean and how did we get here? *Ecosphere, 4*(5), 1–20.

McKeown, R., & United States Teacher Education for Sustainable Development Network. (2013). *Reorienting teacher education to address sustainability: The U.S. context* (White Paper Series, No. 1). Indianapolis, IN: USTESD. Retrieved from https://www.kdp.org/initiatives/pdf/USTESD_WhitePaperOct13.pdf

McKeown, R., & Hopkins, C. (2005). *Guidelines and recommendations for reorienting teacher education to address sustainability* (Technical Paper No. 2). Paris, France: United Nations Education, Scientific, and Cultural Organization. Retrieved from http://unesdoc.unesco.org/images/0014/001433/143370E.pdf

McLean, S. (2013). The whiteness of green: Racialization and environmental education. *The Canadian Geographer/Le Géographe Canadien, 57*(3), 354–362.

Moll, L. C., Amanti, C., Neff, D., & Gonzalez, N. (1992). Funds of knowledge for teaching: Using a qualitative approach to connect homes and classrooms. *Theory Into Practice, 31*(2), 132–141.

National Governors Association Center for Best Practices & Council of Chief State School Officers. (2010). *Common Core State Standards for English language arts.* Washington, DC: NGA, CCSSO.

Newton, P. M. (2015, December). The learning styles myth is thriving in higher education. *Frontiers in Psychology, 6*(1908), 1–5.

Nolet, V. (2009). Preparing sustainability-literate teachers. *Teachers College Record, 111*(2), 409–442.

North American Association for Environmental Education. (1999). *Excellence in environmental education: Guidelines for learning (K–12) – Executive summary and self-assessment tool.* Washington, DC: NAAEE.

Paris, D. (2012). Culturally sustaining pedagogy: A needed change in stance, terminology, and practice. *Educational Researcher, 41*(3), 93–97.

Pellegrini, A. D., & Davis, P. D. (1993). Relations between children's playground and classroom behaviour. *British Journal of Educational Psychology, 63*(1), 88–95.

Pergams, O. R., & Zaradic, P. A. (2008). Evidence for a fundamental and pervasive shift away from nature-based recreation. *Proceedings of the National Academy of Sciences, 105*(7), 2295–2300. Retrieved from http://www.videophilia.org/uploads/PNAScomplete.pdf

Provenzo, E. F., Jr., Renaud, J. P., & Provenzo, A. B. (Eds.). (2009). *Encyclopedia of the social and cultural foundations of education* (Vol. 1). Thousand Oaks, CA: Sage.

Rideout, V. J., Foehr, U. G., & Roberts, D. F. (2005). *Generation M: Media in the lives of 8-to-18 year-olds.* Menlo Park, CA: Henry J. Kaiser Family Foundation.

Rothstein, R. (2008). Whose problem is poverty? *Educational Leadership, 65*(7), 8–13.

Santone, S., & Saunders, S. (2013). Cultivating economic literacy and social wellbeing: An equity perspective. In P. Gorski & J. Landsman (Eds.), *Teaching for class equity and economic justice* (pp. 241–253). Sterling, VA: Stylus.

Sleeter, C. E. (2012). Confronting the marginalization of culturally responsive pedagogy. *Urban Education, 47*(3), 562–584.

Sobel, D. (2004). *Place-based education: Connecting classroom and community.* Barrington, MA: The Orion Society.

Stetsenko, A. (2008). From relational ontology to transformative activist stance on development and learning: Expanding Vygotsky's (CHAT) project. *Cultural Studies of Science Education, 3*(2), 471–491.

Taie, S., & Godring, R. (2017). *Characteristics of public elementary and secondary school teachers in the United States: Results from the 2015–16 national teacher and principal survey, first look.* Washington, DC: National Center for Education Statistics. Retrieved from https://nces.ed.gov/pubsearch/pubsinfo.asp?pubid=2017072

Tomlinson, C. A. (2014). *The differentiated classroom: Responding to the needs of all learners* (2nd ed.). Alexandria, VA: ASCD.

Washington State Institute for Public Policy. (2017). Benefit–cost results. Retrieved from http://www.wsipp.wa.gov/BenefitCost

Wells, N. M., & Lekies, K. S. (2006). Nature and the life course: Pathways from childhood nature experiences to adult environmentalism. *Children, Youth and Environments, 16*(1), 1–24.

Wheeler, R. S. (2008). Becoming adept at code-switching. *Educational Leadership, 65*(7), 54–58.

Woodhouse, J. L., & Knapp, C. E. (2000). *Place-based curriculum and instruction: Outdoor and environmental education approaches.* Charleston, WV: ERIC Clearinghouse on Rural Education and Small Schools. (ED448012)

Zeichner, K. M., & Liston, D. P. (2013). *Reflective teaching: An introduction.* New York, NY: Routledge.

5

THE PERILS FOR STUDENTS IN THE STORY OF MORE

Throughout its history, public education has served many purposes: to safeguard democracy, enculturate immigrants, promote social mobility, and develop a skilled workforce. Schools have been called in as first responders to national crises: Ramp up science education to keep the Soviets at bay in the space race; desegregate schools to ameliorate social inequalities; raise achievement to grow the economy.

This slice of educational history encapsulates the question of "more, better, or both?" raised throughout this book. Should schools bolster the economy or advance equity? Or perhaps that's a false dichotomy. After all, current wisdom tells us that if we raise standards and tighten accountability, we will shore up global competitiveness *and* provide marginalized students with the quality learning opportunities long denied to them. In one fell swoop, the nation will secure its economic future and render inequality a thing of the past. It sounds logical: A better education translates into better jobs and a more prosperous society. It's the ideal combination of More and Better.

But is it? To answer this, we need to look more deeply at who's spinning this narrative. So let's reintroduce our friend Moore from Chapter 2, "The Story of More," a tale based on the idea that economic growth (more) is the pathway to development (better). The premise has worked for Moore, so why shouldn't it work for everyone? And if it works in society, why shouldn't it work in schools?

It's a seductive theory, and over the past few decades, Moore and Friends have convinced many an educator and policymaker that the plan can work. The narrative has galvanized a new purpose of education—preparing students to compete in the global economy—with a promised outcome: equity.

These beliefs have seeped into the DNA of K–12 education, mutating its goals, metrics, and ultimately, the effects on children and society. Classroom practice has also bent to Moore's will, even if it's not evident. Indeed, educators are under such pressure to raise achievement that there's little energy to inter-rogate the forces that backed us into such a tight corner. But we need to, and that is the focus of this chapter. We're going to break through the noise and critically examine several taken-for-granted tenets:

1. Build the curriculum around standards.
2. Celebrate diversity.
3. Teach students grit.

These ideas, like siren songs, entice us with their promise. But if we rush to join the choir, we may drown out the voices we really need to hear: our students'. To unmute them, we need to understand how they were silenced in the first place. So let's start our journey with this question.

How Did We Get Here?

Turn the clock back to 1983, and listen as these words send shock waves across the United States:

> Our Nation is at risk. Our once unchallenged preeminence in com-merce, industry, science, and technological innovation is being overtaken by competitors throughout the world. ... We live among determined, well-educated, and strongly motivated competitors. ... We compete with them for international standing and markets.

Thus tolled the ominous opening of *A Nation at Risk* (para. 1, 6), a sobering account of U.S. decline. Released by the National Commission on Excellence (a federal panel convened under Education Secretary Terrell Bell), the report tallied a litany of failures—from adult illiteracy to dismal K–12 achievement—and laid the blame for the country's alleged downfall at the feet of public education. While skeptics called out the report's overblown rhetoric and unsub-stantiated data, *A Nation at Risk* ignited calls for higher standards and increased accountability—ideas that stuck (Berliner & Biddle, 1995; Goodlad, 2003).

Soon after, in 1991, President George H. W. Bush issued *America 2000: An Education Strategy*, a document that enumerated eight educational goals, in-cluding global preeminence in math and science and the readiness of adults to "compete in a global economy" (p. 64). Notably, the document also integrated democratic goals, such as "making communities places where learning can hap-pen" and "ensur[ing] that all students learn to use their minds well" for citizen-ship as well as employment (p. 57). In this vision, democracy, opportunity, and economic readiness go hand in hand.

As the new century dawned, the demands of the technical economy inten-sified pressures to boost both academic and economic competitiveness based on the belief that the former creates the latter. But with achievement goals still unmet, President George W. Bush signed the 2001 No Child Left Behind Act (NCLB, 2002), making high stakes, standard-based tests the law of the land. "College and career readiness," "21st century skills," and "making students competitive in the global economy" became the new mantras—rhetoric shaped by public–private alliances that gave businesses more seats at the table (Mehta, 2015). Consider the Partnership for 21st Century Skills (P21, now the Partnership for 21st Century Learning). Founded in 2002, P21 (2017) united "the business community, education leaders, and policymakers" to advance a joint agenda of "21st century readiness." To lend a hand, the U.S. Chamber of Commerce (2017) helpfully committed to "fixing shortcomings in our education system."

Achieve, Inc. is another organization that blurred the lines between public and private interests. Founded in 1996 by "leading governors and business leaders," Achieve's (2017) inaugural projects, the 1998 Academic Standards and Assessments Benchmarking Pilot Project and the 2001 American Diploma Project, defined "the 'must-have' knowledge and skills most demanded by higher education and employers." The foundation of this must-have knowledge was a "Common Core of English and mathematics 'benchmarks.'"

Can you guess where this is going?

That's right, Achieve partnered with the National Governors Association (NGA) and the Council of Chief State School Officers (CCSSO) to develop the Common Core State Standards. (Achieve also played a role in developing the Next Generation Science Standards.) Because the federal government is prohibited from dictating standards, funding came from private sources; Achieve and other nonprofits received $233 million from the Gates Foundation alone (Layton, 2014).

The standards were unveiled in 2010 with a fanfare that leaves nothing to the imagination: "With American students fully prepared for the future, our communities will be best positioned to compete successfully in the global economy" (NGA & CCSSO, 2010). Nowhere are these priorities declared more clearly than in the current mission statement of the U.S. Department of Education (DOE): "To promote student achievement and preparation for global competitiveness by fostering educational excellence and ensuring equal access."

The urgency in the discourse feeds the relentless push for technology. And while jobs are essential and businesses are indeed stakeholders in education, the encroachment of private interests has subordinated *equal access* to *competitiveness*. Why doesn't equity come first?

In some ways, it always has—at least in theory. NCLB passed with bipartisan support based on a common recognition of persistent educational disparities; Title I of NCLB, "Improving the Academic Achievement of the Disadvantaged," speaks to this. Civil rights groups including the National Association for the Advancement of Colored People (NAACP) got behind NCLB's accountability provisions, contending that they brought long-neglected inequalities to light (Brown, 2015; Darling-Hammond, 2007). Going back to 1983, *A Nation at Risk* actually started with this statement: "All, regardless of race or class or economic status, are entitled to a fair chance and to the tools for developing their individual powers of mind and spirit to the utmost."

Indeed, the pursuit of equity really never disappeared; it simply took on a new purpose—economic competitiveness—to be achieved through a new solution: higher standards and test-based accountability. In the narrative's cause-effect premise, educational reforms that serve economic growth will fix the nation's long-standing equity problem.

Certainly we all want students to succeed academically, but prevailing policies have whittled down the concept of *success* to sterile data points. The centrality of test scores discounts students' physical, emotional, and social development, much the way the GDP discounts environmental and social costs. As one promising step (noted in Chapter 4), NCLB's successor, the 2015 Every Student Succeeds Act (ESSA) requires states to track a nonacademic metric (e.g., attendance). Yet despite this modification, high-stakes assessments are still the law, based upon standards that fail to account for students' overall well-being. Moreover, indicators to track the health of the community and the environment—education's support systems—are also conspicuously absent, communicating to both students and the public that the only twenty-first-century issues that count are economic ones. It's a myopic view of the future that can leave students blindsided by the other global challenges they will face.

In terms of actual results, the data on inequality presented in Chapter 1 tell us that Moore's educational plan is far from working. And we would be foolish to expect otherwise. Like its parent narrative, the Story of More, current policies profess to eliminate inequality while actually perpetuating and even requiring it. This contradiction creates an educational tragedy that parallels Hardin's cautionary tale (see Chapter 1). Like the herder who encloses the open-access pasture, K–12's coercive "race to the top" gates-off opportunities, granting entry only to the winners—those proven worthy enough to get resources presumed to be scarce. True, physical assets such as classroom space are subject to scarcity, as noted in Chapter 1. However, other opportunity factors—respect, dignity, high expectations—are not subject to such constraints. It doesn't cost anything to believe in students, and respecting one child does not diminish our ability to respect them all. *There's simply no justification for rationing these factors.* Yet the compulsory rivalry goes on, fed by the narrative that your advancement costs mine. The fear drives us to hoard all we can and wrest what's left from our adversaries' hands. As Labaree (1997) described it, "Education has become an investment in my future, not yours, in my children, not other people's children" (p. 48). Like the market, meritocratic testing will efficiently handle the "grading, sorting, and selecting [of] students" so vital to the game (p. 48).

The manufactured pressures have engulfed educators, priming the field to readily accept—rather than cautiously assess—several much-touted practices, starting with this one.

Build the Curriculum Around Standards

The No Child Left Behind Act made high-stakes tests the centerpiece of accountability, driving educators to make standards the basis of instruction. It's a logical response given that rewards and punishments hinge on test results, in particular for language arts and math—the focus of Common Core. But the standards-first movement has sidelined other aspects of instruction, eroding both individual well-being as well as students' connections to the larger world around them.

One impact is a narrowed curriculum. Between 2001 and 2007 (at the height of NCLB), 44% of school districts had cut instructional time in areas such as social studies to increase the focus on language arts and math, the tested subjects (Center on Education Policy, 2007). In addition, a 2010 study found that young children spent far more time on worksheets and direct instruction and less time on drama and arts than their 1998 counterparts did (Bassok, Latham, & Rorem, 2016).

The introduction of Common Core on top of existing testing mandates further altered daily instruction. A host of key shifts in Common Core (NGA & CCSSO, 2017) increased grade-level expectations, especially at younger grades. Kindergarten has been dubbed "the new first grade," with educators questioning whether 5-year-old children are developmentally ready for the literacy and math skills traditionally taught to older students (Bassok et al., 2016; Gewertz, 2010).

Student health has been another casualty of escalating academic pressures. For example, some schools have opted to reduce recess to carve out more time for academics (Caplan & Igel, 2015). This is especially shortsighted given that exercise can improve students' focus and on-task behaviors—let alone the greater goal of children's health (Miller & Almon, 2009). As addressed in Chapter 4, unstructured outdoor play and nature exploration are effective ways to support students' physical wellness while mitigating mental stressors such as ecoanxiety, that is, the sense of dread and hopelessness in the face of mounting environmental problems (Clayton, Manning, Krygsman, & Speiser, 2017). Play also has an embedded equity dimension; a 2005 report from the U.S. DOE revealed that students of color attending high-poverty schools had far less outdoor play time, a "recess gap" that parallels other opportunity gaps. Likewise, low-income children in urban areas are less likely to have safe places for outdoor play, predictably resulting in more TV and other sedentary activities (Kimbro, Brooks-Gunn, & McLanahan, 2011).

As we read in Chapter 4, social-emotional learning (SEL) is one strategy to get student well-being back on the radar. But there's been pushback here, with critics mocking SEL as a feel-good fad. Consider an *Education Week* editorial by the Fordham Institute's Chester Finn. Pulling no punches, Finn (2017) mocked SEL as a "hoax ... rooted in 'faux psychology,'" and then compared it to the self-esteem movement, a largely defunct trend that had its heyday in the 1990s. Finn also took SEL competencies to task for their "feeble mention of ethics" and their silence on morality and other "old-fashioned virtues as integrity, courage, or honesty, and certainly nothing as edgy as patriotism" (para 11). While thoughtful appraisal of SEL is ongoing and necessary, Finn's analysis reveals that he misinterpreted (or simply did not read) the SEL competencies. For example, Finn erroneously assumed that integrity, honesty, and ethics can occur without SEL skills such as responsible decision-making, a competency which (surprise!) includes the "ability to make constructive and respectful choices about personal behavior and social interactions based on consideration of ethical standards" (Collaborative for Academic, Social, and Emotional Learning [CASEL], 2017, para 6). And insofar as patriotism involves civic engagement and social awareness—and not simply blind allegiance—Finn contradicted his own assertion that SEL is not "aimed at citizenship" (para. 12). We can only guess who'll be the first to throw up his hands and blame teachers when Johnny graduates high school without the soft skills sought by employers and therefore can't compete in the job market.

We've seen how prioritizing standards can narrow the curriculum, resulting in a reductionist approach to learning that isolates disciplines from each other—not unlike Bacon's reductionist worldview discussed in Chapter 2. No one questions the importance of language arts and math, but elevating standards above all else keeps learning confined to the classroom and the textbook, sending the message that anything outside of the window or not on the test is superfluous. This deals a blow to the very idea of interdependence and the bonds among schools, communities, and the environment. Consequently, students can come to see their local environment as unrelated to their lives. As we read in Chapter 4, place-based learning can counter this by developing students' identities as members of ecological and social communities. Quality environmental education (EE) can also strengthen students' sense of connection and responsibility to the world around them. But perhaps surprisingly, certain forms of EE can actually exacerbate the illusion of separateness.

Consider lessons that present the environment as a wild, distant place without people—a place to perhaps visit someday. Such framing is not only scientifically inaccurate, but it can also be an affront to spirituality. *Green* curriculum limited to stereotypical topics such as endangered species and the rainforest does little to advance the critical thinking and civic engagement goals of sustainability literacy. Moreover, distancing students from the environment can inadvertently impart the idea that the natural world is at our disposal—the anthropocentric mindset we've discussed. Notably, this worldview is not innate, but is learned and calcifies as children get older (Herrmann, Waxman, & Medin, 2010; Kahn, 1997).

Learning that situates students outside of the community keeps them from fully comprehending the dynamic, life-sustaining setting for their lives and the coactors who share the stage. This hinders students' ability to cultivate an ethos of stewardship their very lives depends upon. Consequently, students are less likely to fully grasp the relevance of local or world events and less inclined to become involved (Sawitri, Hadiyanto, & Hadi, 2015). Disconnection destabilizes democracy as it erodes the social and ecological relationships that support the common good.

Of course, a crucial element of the common good is full inclusion. For educators, this means creating learning environments that provide all students with respect. That leads us to the critique of our next tenet.

Celebrate Diversity

This familiar slogan has saturated the popular culture, inviting us to find joy in our uniqueness and see our pluralistic society as an asset. "Celebrate diversity" has inspired many a workshop, school event, and holiday festivity. It's the legendary stuff of T-shirts, posters, and bumper stickers. But there's one thing diversity isn't: a solution to educational inequities. That takes structural change. But not enough schools have gotten the memo, leaving well-intentioned educators to embrace diversity as a means to *deal with* culture. While our collective backgrounds are indeed worthy of celebration, keeping the conversation there not only diverts attention from institutional discrimination, but it can also diminish learning and exclude students. Let's look at how this can occur through individual teacher actions as well as curriculum as a whole.

As we read in Chapter 4, culturally responsive educators commit to understanding the complexities of students' identities in order to expand learning. But teachers who operate from one-dimensional assumptions and stereotypes can actually inhibit it. Consider a teacher who assigns two *urban* students to write a rap while the rest of the class learns how to craft an analytical essay. Or what about an art teacher who wants to *boost self-esteem* by selectively displaying the artwork of students with *ethnic-sounding names*?

These sadly real examples, while potentially well-meaning, box students into stereotypes that constrict, rather than enrich, academic growth. To avoid this, teachers must create cultural on-ramps that actually lead toward new knowledge and skills. In the writing example, *all* students might examine the linguistic elements of a rap (e.g., word choice, tone, structure) and compare this with the conventions of an essay. The artwork example is just wrong. To catalyze meaningful learning, cultural connections must be solid enough to serve as a platform for growth.

The saying "I'm colorblind" is another good intention gone bad. Differences in skin tone are normal and natural, and feigned colorblindness not only ignores this dimension of a student's identity, but also assumes that color, not bias, is the problem (Derman-Sparks & Phillips, 1997). The ever-popular slogan "I treat everyone the same" likewise misses the mark. Equity is not about creating sameness; it's about creating access. A flight of stairs and a wheelchair ramp present two different entryways into a building, but it's this very difference that provides equal access. To meet the needs of a diverse student body, we must replace the rhetoric of "sameness" with a commitment to meeting students' varied needs.

The content of curriculum as a whole is another place where simply tipping a hat to diversity is both inadequate and detrimental. Books and lessons that appear inclusive can fall short in more subtle ways, requiring us to read between the lines. To examine this, we'll juxtapose the work of E. D. Hirsch, Lisa Delpit (from Chapter 4), and James Banks. While their work goes back to the 1980s and 1990s, it's still relevant because the mindsets and practices are still prevalent—and may be ones you grew up with. Let's start with Hirsch.

In his 1987 book *Cultural Literacy*, Hirsch made the case that knowledge of mainstream culture is the key to academic success, especially for students of color. For Hirsch (2010), mainstream meant the "taken for granted" background (p. 31) that "every American needs to know," as his 1987 book's subtitle declared. To ensure students learn this content, Hirsch (2010) argued for a coherent, "specific, fact-filled knowledge building curriculum" to enlarge students' comprehension of the world (p. 31). In 1986, Hirsch initiated the development of the Core Knowledge Sequence with the input of 145 people from "every region, scholarly discipline, and racial and ethnic group" (Hirsch, 2010, p. 33), resulting in a framework (updated in 2013) designed around "access to the best knowledge available, including knowledge of diverse people and cultures" (Core Knowledge Foundation [CKF], 2013, p. viii). Educators are responding; in New York alone, more than 1,000 schools used the Sequence in the 2013–2014 school year (Tampio, 2016).

Hirsh's framework sounded promising, and even more so when he built the equity case. First, Hirsch acknowledged the dominance of mainstream knowledge and formal English, aspects of the "culture of power" Delpit (1988) introduced to us in Chapter 4. Hirsch, like Delpit, asserted that students must learn these codes to succeed in school and at work, and that educators must explicitly teach them to students who enter the classroom with other "funds of knowledge" (Moll, Amanti, Neff, & Gonzalez, 1992). Moreover, Hirsch and Delpit both called into question reliance on "progressive" pedagogies that emphasize open-ended processes while neglecting the concrete skills students may have yet to acquire (Delpit, 1988, p. 285; Hirsch, 1999). Delpit's work on this topic is even quoted in an essay on the Core Knowledge website (Pondiscio, 2017).

But Hirsch quickly parted ways with a tenet of culturally responsive teaching emphasized by Delpit: that students' ways of knowing and being are just as valid as the power culture, albeit employed in different contexts. As we read about in Chapter 4, teachers can employ code-switching to both honor students' backgrounds and help them acquire the dominant language. But the Sequence trounces this idea and instead subordinates nondominant cultures to the *mainstream* proclaimed superior. James Comer (identified in the Sequence as a Yale professor) schooled us on why this is best for kids:

> Respect for cultural diversity is important but is best achieved when young people have adequate background knowledge of mainstream culture. In order for a truly democratic and economically sound society to be maintained, young people must have access to the best knowledge available so that they can understand the issues, express their viewpoints, and act accordingly.
>
> *(CKF, 2013, p. viii)*

The best available knowledge? Says who? Said Hirsch, in a form of doublespeak honed over decades. In a 1992 essay, he waxed eloquently about U.S. pluralism: "Our blood is ... made up of a thousand noble currents all pouring into one" (para. 4). It sounds as though Hirsch was embracing equality, but just wait. With faux diversity credentials in hand, he threw down the gauntlet and posed citizens with an ominous choice: Will we be "ethnic loyalists" (i.e., Korean- or African-Americans) determined to "preserve [our] own identity against" society? Or will we be "cosmopolitan citizens of the world" who put ethnicity aside, knowing it is "but an accident of history" (para. 10)? For Hirsch, the latter choice is of course "the right one" (para. 8). He then accused the loyalists of sowing strife by defining their "essence" through their culture. Provoking divisiveness, Hirsch added, "If we assert the right of all peoples to their own ethnicity, do we also sanction the ethnic intolerance that characterizes so many cultures?" (para. 14).

The claims are neither substantiated nor logical. First, Hirsch's examples reveal that ethnicity is clearly code for people of color, a proxy that assumes White people are "real Americans" and that ethnicity is a trait only the Others possess (see also Chapter 4). Second, ethnicity is one of many identity factors, and it's pure stereotyping to assume that *ethnic* people define themselves solely on that trait. The dig about intolerance is simply fearmongering—an old scare tactic that's seen a disturbing revival. Finally, the cosmopolitan vs. loyalist dichotomy is a false one; in a diverse society, we will be more successful neighbors and colleagues if we can operate in a variety of cultural environments. A one-way expectation that "they" become more like "us" will not build intercultural fluency.

Hirsch's assimilationist vision was cultural subordination masquerading as the greater good. To better understand how this mindset permeates the Sequence, let's bring in the work of James Banks (1998), a scholar who framed multicultural content integration as a four-stage progression.

In Stage 1, the Heroes and Holidays approach, multicultural content focuses on celebrations (e.g., Cinco de Mayo) or exceptional individuals—those deemed acceptable by the mainstream. For example, a lesson on famous scientists might present George Washington Carver, lauding his academic bootstrapping while staying silent on his motivation to improve the self-sufficiency of impoverished Black farmers.

The next stage in Banks's model is the Ethnic Additive approach. Here, cultural content is more substantial but still "an appendage" to the dominant perspective, which remains unquestioned (Banks, 1998, p. 37). This approach best describes the presentation of multicultural content in Hirsch's Sequence. For example, the kindergarten and first-grade curricula include distinct units on Native Americans; however, learning focuses on "how they lived, what they wore and ate, and the homes they lived in" (CKF, 2013, p. 13). The tribes and their cultures seem as little more than historical curiosities; understanding the "current status of the tribe" is literally the last objective on the list.

With the obligatory Native Americans units out of the way, the path is now clear for the Sequence's real stories, such as Columbus's "Early Exploration and Settlement" and the "Early Exploration of the American West" (CKF, 2013, p. 24). Here, terminology carries meaning; *exploration* suggests a brave expedition, and though we may acknowledge or even admire the pioneering spirit (I certainly wouldn't venture out into the unknown), this framing obscures the exploitation, violence, and displacement that resulted from the celebrated voyages and settlements.

Going deeper, Banks's third stage, the Transformative approach, cocentered the experiences of all actors. As Banks (1998) noted, a unit on the so-called "Westward Expansion" would be reframed as "Two Cultures Meet." This more accurate presentation provides fertile ground to engage students in complex analysis. Students would then carry their analysis into the fourth stage, Social Action, which focuses on real-world applications. For example, older students might review the cultural content in their school's curriculum and make recommendations to administration. Younger students can read different accounts of an event and, with teacher guidance, consider whose story is being told and why that matters.

Unfortunately, the Sequence stifles such inquiry by relegating topics such as immigration and civil rights to isolated history units that sidestep contemporary issues. For example, the immigration unit emphasizes Ellis Island, the Statue of Liberty, and the rights of new citizens. Wonderful; my own grandmother came through Ellis Island. But what of the students up against border walls, immigrant bans, and deportation?

Another subtext of Hirsh's work is that multiculturalism is an intellectual desert, making its inclusion a burdensome concession. Indeed, Hirsch (1992) lamented that even after diversifying the content, "we still face the task of giving all children a good education" (para. 27). Can children not get a good education from learning about their own backgrounds? Apparently not. Hirsch stated, "It will do black American children little good" to learn about their heritage "if they still cannot read and write effectively" (para. 28). Aside from ignoring centuries of intellectual and artistic achievements by Africans and African Americans, Hirsch presumed that multicultural content is incompatible with academic excellence rather than a basis for it.

Our purpose here is to help educators better tackle this looming question: Who controls the narrative in our curriculum—or even belongs in it? In pondering this, bear in mind that neither this book nor Banks's model endorses tossing out Western perspectives. We are not challenging "the canon," but rather the grip it has over learning and the forces that crowned it superior. When we teach Western knowledge and history, we must do so in ways that don't marginalize students. Expecting Others to check their lives at the door hands dominant groups even more control to define whose story is worthy.

More than 20 years after Banks's writing, most curriculum has yet to approach the Social Action stage. Yet anti-racist curriculum is needed more than ever. For example, in 2016, the "Trump Effect" unleashed a torrent of hate speech and intimidation among K–12 students, ranging from swastika graffiti in bathrooms to middle schoolers chanting "build that wall" (Southern Poverty Law Center, 2016). But even teachers committed to social justice may be wary of pushing back out of the fear (or a misconception) that they won't be able to meet standards. But as we've begun to see, many standards (including Common Core) emphasize skills, not specific content. This enables teachers to teach the standards—often in more rigorous ways—using a range of content (Sleeter, 2015).

Hirsch (1987) made a point about the benefits of common knowledge in a diverse society, but we must ask whose knowledge and what understandings? Moving society toward the story we want takes collective effort, so imagine if sustainable food systems, nonviolent conflict resolution, and other concerns were the substance of a shared knowledge base?

To recap, diversity is wonderful and gives us much to cherish. But a diverse society requires more than celebrations or even tolerance. Fulfilling democracy's promise of equity requires changing the dynamics that value some groups above others. Anything less than this—from tokenistic relevance to tacked-on multicultural content—obscures the marginalization that such practices actually perpetuate. The root of the problem is the mindset of zero-sum competition ensconced in the Story of More. Because someone has to win, students must be sufficiently ranked and sorted through a system that allows only the best to succeed. This brings us to our next tenet.

Teach Students Grit

Hard work. Perseverance. Grit. There's no more tried-and-true secret to reach the rags-to-riches American Dream, a narrative fueled by a deep-seeded belief in meritocracy. And for many people, the story has worked. But the ladder of upward mobility is not as scalable as it once was. Data from the Internal Revenue Service has shown that parental income is now the strongest predictor of future income, a reality that reinforces persistent racial wealth gaps (Mitnik, Bryant, Weber, & Grusky, 2015).

Does this mean that hard work doesn't matter? Of course not. But the evidence suggests that academic effort alone is insufficient to overcome the social forces that so strongly link race, zip code, and life outcomes. While we must expect students to give their best, we must also address the barriers that undermine their efforts. But given beliefs drive actions, we must first think about our thinking. In this section, we'll examine the topics of deficit thinking, grit, and dehumanization.

Deficit Thinking

Deficit thinking (introduced in Chapter 2) is a mindset that recasts social problems as individual troubles that result from defective morals or cultures. Deficit thinkers create a template for normality that positions them as *regular* and others as exceptions to that norm. With its focus on implicating defective individuals, the deficit perspective provides educators with a convenient escape from confronting the well-documented structural factors that enclose the Commons of opportunity. Instead, the deficit paradigm drives a constellation of assumptions and behaviors that stymie student success.

One manifestation of deficit thinking is teachers' low expectations of students, a problem that surfaces early. For example, Alvidrez and Weinstein (1999) found that preschool teachers underestimated the intelligence of lower-income children, a belief that strongly predicted students' grade-point averages as well as their scores on the Scholastic Aptitude Test (SAT) taken 14 years later. Likewise, Boser, Wilhelm, and Hanna (2014) showed that low-income high school students, whom teachers believed to be less competent, were 53% less likely to earn a college diploma than their more affluent peers. Wildhagen (2012) reported that teachers perceived African-American students as "putting out less effort" than White peers (p. 1).

Once blaming low achievement on inferior genes was no longer socially acceptable (despite efforts to revive the idea[1]), deficit thinkers turned to new narratives based on cultural deprivation (Ryan, 1971). A prime example is the "culture of poverty," a phrase coined by Lewis (1966) to describe the presumed problematic mindsets, behaviors, and lack of values that he concluded characterize families in poverty. While Lewis's work has long been discredited (Billings, 1974; Carmon, 1985), the ideology lives on in K–12 education, particularly through the work of Ruby Payne. Her wildly popular book *A Framework for Understanding Poverty* (2005) attributed generational poverty to factors such as violence, addiction, and the gendered expectations that men fight and *real* women "take care of their men" (p. 59). With more than 1.5 million copies sold (according to her website), the book has positioned Payne as *the* poverty expert, driving a lucrative consulting business, aha! Processes, Inc. While many scholars have blasted Payne's grotesque stereotyping and baseless conclusions, Payne's disciplines tout the script that poverty is a choice, meaning that only good middle-class values can fix these broken individuals (Gorski, 2008; Osei-Kofi, 2005). When applied to pedagogy (see Chapter 4), such mindsets make democratic education and place-based learning all but impossible: Why would a teacher engage students' communities and voices when both are considered defective?

Grit

Deficit-based interventions picked up steam through the concept of grit. Popularized by Angela Duckworth (a MacArthur "Genius" grant recipient), *grit* referred to "perseverance and passion toward long-term goals" (Duckworth & Quinn, 2009, p. 166). Duckworth's research focused on (among other topics) grit's influence on the success of West Point candidates and National Spelling Bee competitors. While grit was never intended as *the* explanation for student underachievement, schools seized upon the concept, spawning a minor industry of grit curriculum, workshops, worksheets, and how-to articles promoted through popular websites such as Edutopia. Cautions and caveats were offered, but were overshadowed by the power and promise of the buzzword.

So is grit the panacea everyone hoped for? Not quite. A meta-analysis of more than 80 studies found that the effect of grit on academic achievement has been overstated (Credé, Tynan, & Harms, 2017). Duckworth and Yeager (2015) also completed a meta-analysis that found a correlation—but no compelling evidence of causation—between executive function ("a suite of top-down cognitive processes," p. 238) and student achievement in reading and math. Moreover, Duckworth herself voiced opposition to measuring grit as part of high-stakes character assessments (Duckworth & Yaeger, 2015).

Healthy skepticism about grit is crucial when the discourse centers on students in poverty. Foregrounding the alleged lack of character diverts attention from structural inequalities and overlooks the tremendous effort it takes to get through the day without adequate food, shelter, or health care—examples of Adverse Childhood Experiences (ACEs), introduced in Chapter 1. And, even if educators acknowledge structural barriers, there's the danger of applauding poverty as a character-building opportunity (Gorski, 2016). We can cheer on kids, feeling good about raising the bar without razing the wall that stands in the way. Grit is likewise cold comfort for students suffering the health effects of environmental toxins. Author Mike Rose noted,

> Can you imagine the outcry if, let's say, an old toxic dump was discovered near Scarsdale or Beverly Hills and the National Institutes of Health undertook a program to teach kids strategies to lessen the effects of the toxins but didn't do anything to address the toxic dump itself?
>
> *(quoted in Strauss & Ris, 2016, para 13)*

There is certainly immense value in persistence and resilience. But chastising sick or traumatized students for "ungrittiness" dismisses the immediacy of their survival needs. For a child who fears yet another beating, getting through the night unharmed *is* a long-term goal. Moreover, even when students engage in clearly unacceptable behaviors, punishments alone are unlikely to be successful without other interventions such as counseling (Flannery, 2016). The point is not to excuse inappropriate actions, but rather to address their root causes. It's the difference between asking, "What's wrong with those kids?" and "What's going on with them?" The former assigns blame; the latter invites a solution.

In Chapter 6, we'll examine a related concept: growth mindset.

Dehumanization

Deficit thinking can also manifest as dehumanization (introduced in Chapter 2), a vestige of the Social Darwinist narrative that asserts genetic hierarchies among humans.

The association of Black people with apes and gorillas is a persistent form of dehumanization with roots in colonialism (Mills & Hund, 2016). The "science" text *Types of Mankind* (Nott & Gliddon, 1854) compared facial illustrations of Europeans, Africans, and gorillas in an attempt to demonstrate the closer biological relationship of the latter two. These ugly associations have persisted, reinforced through policing, the justice systems, and media (Goff, Eberhardt, Williams, & Jackson, 2008). For example, in the early 1990s, California police described crimes involving Blacks as NHI (no humans involved; Wynter, 1992). In addition, news coverage about convicted Blacks is more likely to include ape references than are articles about White convicts (Goff et al., 2008). More recently, Darren Wilson, the police officer responsible for the 2014 shooting of Michael Brown (an unarmed Black teenager) testified that Brown's "intense aggressive face" made him look like "a demon" (Boswell, 2014, para 2); a grand jury declined to bring charges.

When applied to children, these biases have destructive consequences. For example, a set of studies demonstrated that individuals viewed Black children as less innocent and childlike than their White peers (Goff, Jackson, Di Leone, Culotta, & DiTomasso, 2014). These distorted perceptions have followed children and "predicted actual racial disparities in police violence" toward them (Goff et al., 2014, p. 526). The U.S. Government Accountability Office ([GAO], 2018) reported that African-American students represent 15% of the K–12 population, but comprise 31% of students referred to police or arrested at school—a 5% increase over just two schools years (2013–2014 to 2015–2016). And the disproportionalities start early. For example, the U.S. Department of Education Office for Civil Rights (2014) reported that African-American students represent 19% of preschool enrollment, but 48% of students suspended more than once. One could dismiss this by concluding that Black children misbehave more, but schools have historically doled out harsher and more frequent punishments to Blacks (and Latinos) for the same offenses committed by White students (McFadden, Marsh, Prince, & Hwang, 1992; Okonofua & Eberhardt, 2015; Shaw & Braden, 1990; Skiba et al., 2011).

These punitive mindsets creep into school climate, impairing teacher-student relationships, students' sense of engagement, and ultimately, achievement. Conversely, a supportive and respectful climate improves learning outcomes, even tempering the effects of poverty (Berkowitz, Moore, Astor, & Benbenishty, 2017). Recognizing the power of the hidden curriculum, some schools are turning to interventions such as restorative practices, an approach to discipline that focuses on repairing harm (Costello, Wachtel, & Wachtel, 2009).

The falsehoods embedded within deficit scripts have a flipside in the narrative surrounding hierarchy. As the story goes, those at the top made it due to initiative, a virtue that makes them fundamentally different (better) than the Others. This belief normalizes inequality and also absolves the "winners" from further contact with Them, aside from pity or self-affirming benevolence.

It's a powerful creed, and elite students who cling to it enjoy the luxury of remaining oblivious to the dynamics that advantage them (Swalwell, 2013). For example, studies have indicated that wealthy individuals are more inclined than their lower-income peers to espouse beliefs in independence and meritocracy, yet less inclined to demonstrate empathy (Khan, 2011; Stellar, Manzo, Kraus, & Keltner, 2012). And while economically elite students demonstrate greater understanding of civic processes, their public involvement is more likely to focus on individual acts of charity rather than actions that challenge the status quo (Hernández-Sheets, 2000; Swalwell, 2015). To become justice-oriented citizens, *all* students must understand the often hidden forces that structure class relationships (Westheimer & Kahne, 2004). Critical pedagogy is one strategy to develop such consciousness, as we'll examine further in Chapter 6.

Chapter Takeaways

We've dissected seemingly disparate topics to reveal common, root mindsets: zero-sum competition and hierarchy—the driving forces of the Story of More. We've looked at how these mindsets have crept into policies, curriculum, and classroom practice. Here's a summary:

- In a democracy, equal opportunity should be accessible to all, yet dogged inequalities tell us it's not.
- Over the past decades, the narrative of education has morphed into the belief that preparing students to be globally competitive will yield equity.
- As federal policies, NCLB and ESSA have been embraced for illuminating inequalities yet critiqued for the punitive testing that allocates rewards and penalties based on them.

- Increased pressure to raise achievement has prioritized tested subjects at the expense of other disciplines and students' overall well-being.
- Narrowing the curriculum isolates students from ecological and social communities, undermining sustainability.
- Achieving equity requires systemic interventions; however, certain approaches to multiculturalism can reinforce stereotypes and exclusion.
- Deficit ideologies, low expectations, and dehumanization further undermine equity through inaccurate conceptions of students that limit opportunities.
- It is right to expect students to give their best efforts, but we must attend to structural factors beyond their control.

The current educational paradigm is hampering equity, academic achievement, and sustainability literacy. Most importantly, the policies and practices described in this chapter impede students in their journey to shape the future they want. Clearly, it's time for an educational system that reinvigorates democracy, supports the whole student, and puts the creation of sustainable and equitable communities at the center of practice. Chapter 6 offers practical tools and strategies to realize these goals.

Note

1 The patent falsehood of genetic hierarchy has not deterred efforts to revive the theory. For example, the *The Bell Curve: Intelligence and Class Structure* (Hernstein & Murray, 1994) compared IQ scores (itself a contested concept) to assert innate differences in intelligence among races. The authors used their findings (now discredited) to advocate for shifting public resources away from the "less intelligent" (who can only go so far) and toward the "cognitively elite" (read: upper-income Whites).

References

Achieve. (2017). *Read a brief history of Achieve*. Retrieved from https://www.achieve.org/history-achieve

Alvidrez, J., & Weinstein, R. S. (1999). Early teacher perceptions and later student academic achievement. *Journal of Educational Psychology, 91*(4), 731–746.

Banks, J. (1998). Approaches to multicultural curriculum reform. In E. Lee, D. Menkart, & M. Okazawa-Rey (Eds.), *Beyond heroes and holidays: A practical guide to K-12 anti-racist, multicultural education and staff development* (pp. 73–74). Washington, DC: Network of Educators on the Americas.

Bassok, D., Latham, S., & Rorem, A. (2016). Is kindergarten the new first grade? *AERA Open, 1*(4), 1–31.

Berkowitz, R., Moore, H., Astor, R. A., & Benbenishty, R. (2017). A research synthesis of the associations between socioeconomic background, inequality, school climate, and academic achievement. *Review of Educational Research, 87*(2), 425–469.

Berliner, D. C., & Biddle, B. J. (1995). *The manufactured crisis: Myths, fraud, and the attack on America's public schools*. New York, NY: Perseus Books.

Billings, D. (1974). Culture and poverty in Appalachia: A theoretical discussion and empirical analysis. *Social Forces, 53*(2), 315–323.

Boser, U., Wilhelm, M., & Hanna, R. (2014). *The power of the Pygmalion effect: Teachers' expectations strongly predict college completion.* Washington, DC: Center for American Progress.

Boswell, F. (2014, November 26). In Darren Wilson's testimony, familiar themes about Black men. *National Public Radio.* Retrieved from https://www.npr.org/sections/codeswitch/2014/11/26/366788918/in-darren-wilsons-testimony-familiar-themes-about-black-men

Brown, E. (2015, January 12). Civil rights groups back standardized testing in No Child Left Behind rewrite. *The Washington Post.* Retrieved from https://www.washingtonpost.com/local/education/civil-rights-groups-back-standardized-testing-in-no-child-left-behind-rewrite/2015/01/12/511c99e4-99fd-11e4-a7ee-526210d665b4_story.html?utm_term=.f19611a356ce

Bush, G. (1991). *America 2000: An education strategy, Sourcebook.* Washington, DC: U.S. Department of Education.

Caplan, A. L., & Igel, L. H. (2015, January 15). *The Common Core is taking away kids' recess— and that makes no sense.* Retrieved from the Forbes website: https://www.forbes.com/sites/leeigel/2015/01/15/the-common-core-is-taking-away-kids-recess-and-that-makes-no-sense/#2e728d9e128d

Carmon, N. (1985). Poverty and culture: Empirical evidence and implications for public policy. *Sociological Perspectives, 28*(4), 403–417.

Center on Education Policy. (2007, July 25). *As the majority of school districts spend more time on reading and math, many cut time in other areas* [News release]. Washington, DC: Author.

Clayton, S., Manning, C., Krygsman, K., & Speiser, M. (2017). *Mental health and our changing climate: Impacts, implications, and guidance.* Washington, DC: American Psychological Association and ecoAmerica.

Collaborative for Academic, Social, and Emotional Learning. (2017). *Core SEL competencies.* Retrieved from http://www.casel.org/social-and-emotional-learning/core-competencies

Core Knowledge Foundation. (2013). *Core knowledge sequence: Content and skill guidelines for grades K–8.* Charlottesville, VA: Core Knowledge Foundation.

Costello, B., Wachtel, J., & Wachtel, T. (2009). *The restorative practices handbook for teachers, disciplinarians and administrators: Building a culture of community in schools.* Bethlehem, PA: International Institute for Restorative Practices.

Credé, M., Tynan, M. C., & Harms, P. D. (2017). Much ado about grit: A meta-analytic synthesis of the grit literature. *Journal of Personality and Social Psychology, 113*(3), 492–511.

Darling-Hammond, L. (2007). Evaluating "No Child Left Behind." *The Nation, 284*(20), 11–21.

Delpit, L. D. (1988). The silenced dialogue: Power and pedagogy in educating other people's children. *Harvard Educational Review, 58*(3), 280–298.

Derman-Sparks, L., & Phillips, C. B. (1997). *Teaching/learning anti-racism: A developmental approach.* New York, NY: Teachers College Press.

Duckworth, A. L., & Quinn, P. D. (2009). Development and validation of the Short Grit Scale (GRIT–S). *Journal of Personality Assessment, 91*(2), 166–174.

Duckworth, A. L., & Yeager, D. S. (2015). Measurement matters: Assessing personal qualities other than cognitive ability for educational purposes. *Educational Researcher, 44*(4), 237–251.

Every Student Succeeds Act, Pub. L. No. 114–95 § 1002, Stat. 1802 (2015).

Finn, C. E., Jr. (2017, June 19). Why are schools still peddling the self-esteem hoax? *Education Week*. Retrieved from https://www.edweek.org/ew/articles/2017/06/21/why-are-schools-still-peddling-the-self-esteem.html

Flannery, M. E. (2016, November 3). *How schools are helping traumatized students learn again*. Retrieved from http://neatoday.org/2016/11/03/schools-helping-traumatized-students

Gewertz, C. (2010, December 6). Study: Most students fail to meet common-standards bar. *Education Week*. Retrieved from https://www.edweek.org/ew/articles/2010/12/06/15standards.h30.html

Goff, P. A., Eberhardt, J. L., Williams, M. J., & Jackson, M. C. (2008). Not yet human: Implicit knowledge, historical dehumanization, and contemporary consequences. *Journal of Personality and Social Psychology, 94*(2), 292–306.

Goff, P. A., Jackson, M. C., Di Leone, B. A. L., Culotta, C. M., & DiTomasso, N. A. (2014). The essence of innocence: Consequences of dehumanizing Black children. *Journal of Personality and Social Psychology, 106*(4), 526–545.

Goodlad, J. I. (2003, April 2003). A nation in wait. *Education Week*. Retrieved from https://www.edweek.org/ew/articles/2003/04/23/32goodlad.h22.html

Gorski, P. C. (2008). Peddling poverty for profit: Elements of oppression in Ruby Payne's framework. *Equity & Excellence in Education, 41*(1), 130–148.

Gorski, P. C. (2016). Poverty and the ideological imperative: A call to unhook from deficit and grit ideology and to strive for structural ideology in teacher education. *Journal of Education for Teaching, 42*(4), 378–386.

Hernández-Sheets, R. (2000). Advancing the field or taking center stage: The white movement in multicultural education [Book Reviews]. *Educational Researcher, 29*(9), 15–21.

Hernstein, R., & Murray, C. (1994). *The bell curve: Intelligence and class structure in American life*. New York, NY: Simon & Shuster.

Herrmann, P., Waxman, S. R., & Medin, D. L. (2010). Anthropocentrism is not the first step in children's reasoning about the natural world. *Proceedings of the National Academy of Sciences, 107*(22), 9979–9984.

Hirsch, E. D., Jr. (1987). *Cultural literacy: What every American needs to know*. Boston, MA: Houghton Mifflin.

Hirsch, E. D., Jr. (1992). *Toward a centrist curriculum: Two kinds of multiculturalism in elementary school*. Charlottesville, VA: Core Knowledge Foundation.

Hirsch, E. D., Jr. (1999, October). *Why core knowledge promotes social justice* (Convocation address to students and faculty of the University of Tennessee–Chattanooga,). Retrieved from https://www.coreknowledge.org/about-us/e-d-hirsch-jr/articles-e-d-hirsch-jr

Hirsch, E. D., Jr. (2010). Beyond comprehension: We have yet to adopt a Common Core curriculum that builds knowledge grade by grade—but we need to. *American Educator, 34*(4), 30–36.

Kahn, Jr., P. H. (1997). Children's moral and ecological reasoning about the Prince William Sound oil spill. *Developmental Psychology, 33*(6), 1091–1096.

Khan, S. (2011). *Privilege: The making of an adolescent elite at St. Paul's School*. Princeton, NJ: Princeton University Press.

Kimbro, R. T., Brooks-Gunn, J., & McLanahan, S. (2011). Young children in urban areas: Links among neighborhood characteristics, weight status, outdoor play, and television watching. *Social Science & Medicine, 72*(5), 668–676.

Labaree, D. F. (1997). Public goods, private goods: The American struggle over educational goals. *American Educational Research Journal, 34*(1), 39–81.

Layton, L. (2014, June 7). How Bill Gates pulled off the swift Common Core revolution. *The Washington Post.* Retrieved from https://www.washingtonpost.com/politics/how-bill-gates-pulled-off-the-swift-common-core-revolution/2014/06/07/a830e32e-ec34-11e3-9f5c-9075d5508f0a_story.html?utm_term=.48fde4271763

Lewis, O. (1966). *La vida: A Puerto Rican family in the culture of poverty–San Juan and New York.* New York, NY: Random House.

McFadden, A. C., Marsh, G. E., II, Price, B. J., & Hwang, Y. (1992). A study of race and gender bias in the punishment of school children. *Education and Treatment of Children, 15*(2), 140–146.

Mehta, J. (2015). Escaping the shadow: *A Nation at Risk* and its far-reaching influence. *American Educator, 39*(2), 20–26, 44.

Miller, E., & Almon, J. (2009). *Crisis in the kindergarten: Why children need to play in school.* College Park, MD: Alliance for Childhood.

Mills, C. W., & Hund, W. D. (2016, February 28). Africa: Comparing Black people to monkeys has a long, dark simian history. *The Conversation.* Retrieved from http://theconversation.com/comparing-black-people-to-monkeys-has-a-long-dark-simian-history-55102

Mitnik, P., Bryant, V., Weber, M., & Grusky, D. B. (2015). *New estimates of intergenerational mobility using administrative data* (SOI Working Paper). Washington, DC: Statistics of Income Division, Internal Revenue Service.

Moll, L. C., Amanti, C., Neff, D., & Gonzalez, N. (1992). Funds of knowledge for teaching: Using a qualitative approach to connect homes and classrooms. *Theory Into Practice, 31*(2), 132–141.

National Governors Association Center for Best Practices & Council of Chief State School Officers. (2010). *Common Core State Standards for English language arts.* Washington, DC: NGA, CCSSO.

National Governors Association Center for Best Practices, Council of Chief State School Officers. (2017). *Key shifts in English language arts.* Washington, DC: NGA, CCSSO. Retrieved from http://www.corestandards.org/other-resources/key-shifts-in-english-language-arts

No Child Left Behind Act of 2001, Public L. 107–110, §115 Stat. 1425, codified as amended at 20 U.S.C. §6301 (2002).

Nott, J., & Gliddon, G. (1854). *Types of mankind.* Philadelphia, PA: Lippincott, Grambo & Co.

Okonofua, J. A., & Eberhardt, J. L. (2015). Two strikes: Race and the disciplining of young students. *Psychological Science, 26*(5), 617–624.

Osei-Kofi, N. (2005). Pathologizing the poor: A framework for understanding Ruby Payne's work. *Equity and Excellence in Education, 38*(4), 367–375.

Partnership for 21st Century Learning. (2017). *Our history.* Retrieved from http://www.p21.org/about-us/our-history

Payne, R. K. (2005). *A framework for understanding poverty* (4th ed.). Highlands, TX: aha! Process, Inc.

Pondiscio, R. (2017, July 14). *Cultural literacy and the language of upward mobility.* Retrieved from https://www.coreknowledge.org/blog/cultural-literacy-language-upward-mobility

Ryan, W. (1971). *Blaming the victim.* New York, NY: Vintage Books.

Sawitri, D. R., Hadiyanto, H., & Hadi, S. P. (2015). Pro-environmental behavior from a socialcognitive theory perspective. *Procedia Environmental Sciences, 23*, 27–33.

Shaw, S. R., & Braden, J. P. (1990). Race and gender bias in the administration of corporal punishment. *School Psychology Review, 19*(3), 378–383.

Skiba, R. J., Horner, R. H., Chung, C. G., Rausch, M. K., May, S. L., & Tobin, T. (2011). Race is not neutral: A national investigation of African American and Latino disproportionality in school discipline. *School Psychology Review, 40*(1), 85–107.

Sleeter, C. (2015, June 18). *Standards and multicultural education.* Retrieved from http://christinesleeter.org/standards-and-multicultural

Southern Poverty Law Center. (2016, November 29). *Ten days after: Harassment and intimidation in the aftermath of the election.* Retrieved from https://www.splcenter.org/20161129/ten-days-after-harassment-and-intimidation-aftermath-election

Stellar, J. E., Manzo, V. M., Kraus, M. W., & Keltner, D. (2012). Class and compassion: Socioeconomic factors predict responses to suffering. *Emotion, 12*(3), 449–459.

Strauss, V., & Ris, E. (2016, May 10). The problem with teaching 'grit' to poor kids? They already have it. Here's what they really need. *The Washington Post.*

Swalwell, K. (2015). Mind the civic empowerment gap: Economically elite students and critical civic education. *Curriculum Inquiry, 45*(5), 491–512.

Swalwell, K. M. (2013). *Educating activist allies: Social justice pedagogy with the suburban and urban elite.* New York, NY: Routledge.

Tampio, N. (2016, July 7). The false promise of core knowledge. *Huffington Post.* Retrieved from https://www.huffingtonpost.com/nicholas-tampio/the-false-promise-of-core_b_7739000.html

U.S. Chamber of Commerce. (2017). *Education.* Retrieved from https://www.uschamber.com/education

U.S. Department of Education Office for Civil Rights. (2014, March). *Civil rights data collection. Data snapshot: School discipline* (Issue Brief No. 1). Retrieved from https://ocrdata.ed.gov/downloads/crdc-school-discipline-snapshot.pdf

U.S. Government Accountability Office. (2018). *K–12 education: Discipline disparities for Black students, boys, and students with disabilities.* Washington, DC: Author.

Westheimer, J., & Kahne, J. (2004). What kind of citizen? The politics of educating for democracy. *American Educational Research Journal, 41*(2), 237–269.

Wildhagen, T. (2012). How teachers and schools contribute to racial differences in the realization of academic potential. *Teachers College Record, 114*(7), 1–27.

Wynter, S. (1992). "No humans involved": An open letter to my colleagues. *Voices of the African Diaspora, 8*, 1–17.

6

BEST PRACTICES FOR STUDENT SUCCESS IN THE STORY OF BETTER

Educating for sustainability and social justice is about the kind of citizens we create and the kind of world they'll create together. To make a life for themselves, students will need to replace the ecological and social crises they'll inherit with a story of sustainability and social justice. But what knowledge and skills will prepare students? What values will guide them? And how do we begin organizing our curriculum to enable this? This chapter will answer these questions.

In Chapter 4, we introduced pedagogical guidelines for sustainability and social justice. In Chapter 5, we exposed some of the contradictory mindsets and practices. This chapter outlines essential learning outcomes and instructional strategies, supported by examples across grades and disciplines. In the Culminating Activity that follows this chapter, you'll apply all you've learned to evaluate the specific unit or course you intend to reframe in Part III.

This chapter is organized around the three common domains of competencies—the "head, hands, and heart" of learning (Sipos, 2009):

- Knowledge: What "literacies" do students need to understand the world?
- Skills: What specific competencies do students need to improve their lives and communities?
- Dispositions: What are the mindsets and orientations that will provide the compass?

Comprehensive lists of sustainability "standards" for these domains have been defined in prior literature (Cloud, 2016; Nolet, 2013); Table 6.1 provides a sampling.

TABLE 6.1 Examples of Student Competencies

Content knowledge	Skills	Dispositions
Environmental literacy	Perspective-taking	Gratitude
Diversity and culture	Critical thinking	Empathy
Community design	Decision-making and	Ethics
Energy	problem-solving	Social consciousness
Food	Systems thinking	Respect for others
Health	Intercultural communication	Commitment to the
The economy	Technological literacy	common good
Transportation	Creativity	Agency and efficacy
Water	Life skills (e.g., gardening)	
	Conflict resolution	

Content Knowledge: What Do Students Need to Know?

Content is arguably the substance of the curriculum, so let's introduce two approaches for integrating sustainability and social justice: (a) teaching about clearly related topics; and (b) reframing your existing topics through the lenses of the foundational concepts we've covered, such as interdependence and community. (See the Part I Culminating Activity.)

1. In the first approach, "low hanging fruit" topics such as climate change, food system, and social movements serve as the plots at the center of instruction. This method works well if such topics are naturally part of your discipline.
2. In contrast, the second approach applies the foundational concepts to reframe *any* topic. This method works well for content that at first blush seems unrelated to sustainability and social justice. (See the Part I Culminating Activity to review the concepts.)

While the methods are different, they both focus inquiry on the "real and immediate conditions" of students' lives, preparing them for effective and ethical social engagement (Duncan-Andrade, 2007, p. 627). And, while we know it's possible to teach about sustainability as an academic topic divorced from real-world applications (e.g., study climate change but then close the book and return to business as usual), this chapter and those ahead will ensure that reframing your curriculum leads to intentional action.

Let's take a closer look at each method.

Content Integration Method 1: Teach Topics Clearly Related to Sustainability and Social Justice

Topics such as food and water offer clear opportunities to create units and courses focused on "an explicit intent to solve problems that are complex and multidimensional, especially those that involve an interface of human and natural systems" (Wickson, Carew, & Russell, 2006, p. 1048). This is the basis of transdisciplinary curriculum, which organizes content based on the ways it's experienced, leading to solutions that transcend disciplinary boundaries (Costanza, 1990). For example, remediating a brownfield (e.g., a contaminated property) unifies ecology, engineering, hydrology, public policy, environmental justice, and more. Disciplinary expertise is enhanced, not diluted, in the service of the solution. And, with its focus on civic engagement, transdisciplinary learning supports democratic education.

Here's a "top 10" list of transdisciplinary topics with framing questions (presented alphabetically):

1. Community planning: How can we design healthy, safe, sustainable communities where all can thrive?
2. Conflict resolution: How can we resolve differences in ways that are peaceful and beneficial to all?
3. Consumption: How can we meet our material needs within the constraints of the environment, while also supporting shared prosperity?
4. Diversity: How are different forms of diversity (e.g., cultural, biological) related? How can we communicate and work in multiple cultural contexts?
5. Ecological sustainability: What are ways individuals and societies can steward and restore ecosystems?
6. The economy: How can we structure economic and financial systems that support ecological sustainability and equity?
7. Energy: How can we meet growing energy needs in ways that sustain ecosystems, provide livelihoods, and ensure equity?
8. Food: How can we create a food system that nourishes people, communities, economies, and cultures?
9. Health care: What does it take to maintain physical and mental health as individuals and a society?
10. Water: How can we provide equitable access to clean water?

While a transdisciplinary approach is an ideal, the reality is that the structure of courses often reinforces (and even rewards) disciplinary specialization. Instructors thus need to find ways to "stretch" content without undermining it. To help you visualize possibilities, the book's website offers resources that apply the preceding topics across disciplines and grades. Even if you are not going to teach this specific content, the resources may spark ideas.

Content Integration Method 2: Reframe Topics Through the Foundational Concepts of Sustainability and Social Justice

Our "top 10" list offers content that easily drives strong plots. But what if your required content seems far removed from such issues? Maybe you're teaching forces and motion in physics or linear equations in math. Where's the plot—and how can you formulate one without abandoning standards or requirements? This is where our second method comes in: reframing your existing topics using the foundational concepts (shown again in Table 6.2 that follows). These concepts are powerful because they are transferable across disciplines, inject significance, and surface what's at stake.

A unit on rocks and minerals, for example, might cover geographical distribution, chemical formulas, or uses of coal. Learning emphasizes facts, figures, and formulas. It's useful information, but the "neutral" presentation obscures what's really at stake. To unearth the plot, overlay the concepts of *equity* and *limits* and compelling new questions emerge. Does the mining and consumption of [this material] work within the constraints of the ecosystem? What are the implications of how we manufacture, use, and dispose of these materials? What are the impacts on miners and communities? Now the stakes are evident: the combined well-being of the community, workers, and the environment. The unit covers mandated content, but problematizes it based on real concerns.

So which concepts should you reach for? Table 6.2 can help you choose. The left-hand column lists the foundational concepts addressed throughout this book. The other columns show the intersection of each concept with different disciplines. To generate ideas for your own curriculum, choose several concepts that seem most relevant and then read across to find the connections. In Chapter 7, you'll return to the table to reframe your unit or course.

Skills and Dispositions

The content we've described gives us a plot, but it takes skills and mindsets to move knowledge into action. As students work to solve the challenge before them, they play many roles: an informed citizen, an ethical decision-maker, a skilled communicator, a geographer and historian, and a loving family member, to name a few. Given that full coverage on these roles is beyond the scope of the book, we will focus on "meta" proficiencies that transcend grades and disciplines:

- Systems thinking;
- Empathy, social consciousness, and critical thinking;
- Equity-literate communication skills;
- Self-efficacy and agency; and
- Creativity.

TABLE 6.2 Foundational Concepts Applied Across Disciplines

Defining concept	Sciences/math	Social sciences/law	Humanities/language	Business/economics	Arts/communication
Beauty	Elegance in the math, sound, music, and natural phenomena	Cultural influences on definitions, perceptions, and aesthetics	Representations of beauty in literature, religion, and philosophy	Aesthetics of design, implications of commodifying beauty	Biophilia (affinity for nature's beauty)
Change	Change as a condition of life, history of scientific and mathematical knowledge	The evolution of legal and social structures, changing conceptions of justice	The role of communication in sustainability and social justice	Business cycles, policies to change economic paradigms	The reciprocal relationship between arts and social change
Community	Sustainable communities: land use, water, green roofs, etc.	Equitable housing, gentrification, community policing, restorative justice	Community history, folklore, and traditions	Community currencies, time banks, micro-lending, fair trade	Public art and murals, the role of art in sustainable communities
Diversity	Biological diversity, genetic engineering, epistemology, diverse ways of knowing	Creating equitable social institutions, cross-cultural conflict resolution	History and literature from multiple perspectives, power, privilege, and language	Full-cost accounting that incorporates the value of diversity	Diversity in artistic expression and representation in "the cannon"
Ecological sustainability	Ecological footprinting, permaculture, appropriate technology	Environmental psychology, biophilia, legal rights of nature	Cultural influences on sustainability, sustainability (or not) in past civilizations	Biomimicry, circular design, life cycle analysis	Representations of nature in different art forms/genres/periods, use of natural art materials

(Continued)

Defining concept	Sciences/math	Social sciences/law	Humanities/language	Business/economics	Arts/communication
Equity/ethics	Ethics of science, racial/socioeconomic health disparities	Creating equitable systems of justice and policing	Comparative analysis of ethics and values across civilizations, eras, etc.	Business ethics, equitable access to capital	Equitable representation of diverse artists, equitable access to arts-related opportunities
Interdependence	STEM as part of transdiciplinary thinking	Healthy human-environmental relationships, the evolution of prosocial inclinations, biophilia	Influence of literature, linguistics, religion, and philosophy on environmental thinking	Interdependence of economic, ecological, and social systems	The arts' role in strengthening relationships among people and communities
Limits/scale	Respecting ecological limits in applications of STEM	Scaling human society to promote strong social structures	Analyzing the assumptions in terms such as *development*	Optimizing the scale of the economy	Representations of human or environmental limits
Resilience	Modeling resilience in complex systems	Social structures that support resiliency in people and communities	Historical examples of community and cultural resiliency	Developing resilient economic and financial systems	Arts to support emotional resilience
Systems	Using systems modeling to solve sustainability challenges	Fostering just social institutions	Interdependence of the cultural and ecological Commons	Relationship among social, economic, and ecological systems; feedback loops; unintended consequences	Performing arts ensembles as systems
Well-being	Applications of science to promote well-being (nutrition, etc.)	Ways social structures and institutions can support well-being	The role of literature, linguistics, and religion in sustaining cultures and communities	Business models, products, and services that support well-being	The arts' role in supporting personal, social, and cultural well-being

Examples throughout this section will reinforce the inseparability of knowledge, skills, and dispositions. As we'll see, students cannot think critically about one-dimensional content that offers nothing to question, probe, or ponder. Nor can they make ethical decisions about topics presented as value-neutral.

Let's get started.

Learning to See Wholeness: Systems Thinking

If we had to sum up this book in one concept, it would be (wait for it) interdependence. We know from Chapter 1 that nothing exists in isolation; this includes students, who must learn to see themselves as members of ecological and social communities. Place-based education, described in Chapter 4, is one way to foster this relationship-based view of the world. This is a pillar of systems thinking, a way of understanding based on wholeness and connections.

To review, a system is a group of interacting, interrelated, or interdependent *elements* forming a complex whole; examples include ecosystems and educational systems (which are nested in the former). Systems can be comprised of living and/or nonliving elements that together have a function or purpose. While the parts can be examined independently, the overall systems can be understood only through the interactions.

Thorough explanations of systems-thinking vocabulary can be found in other literature (Meadows, 2008; Sweeney & Meadows, 2010). Readers are encouraged to consult those resources for in-depth analysis. But to provide immediate applications, we'll introduce some strategies to teach fundamental concepts including interdependence, connections, change, and cycles. As you read, consider how you might adapt the ideas for your grade and discipline.

Constructing an ecosystems web is a classic activity to teach interdependence to young children (or students of any age). Start by giving each student a "name tag" with an ecosystem element (e.g., trees, grass, bird), and arrange students in a circle. The teacher, who represents the sun, has a ball of yarn. Holding onto the loose end, he or she announces, "My sunlight provides food for …," and then tosses the ball to the "tree" so that they are connected. That student (directed by the teacher as needed) states another connection ("I provide habitat for the bird"), holds onto his or her end of the yarn, and tosses the ball to the appropriate student. As the activity continues, a web takes form. To emphasize the vital role of each element, have a few students drop their end of the yarn and ask the class what happens (it falls apart). You can also apply the principle to the classroom: Just as species in the ecosystem are interdependent, students in a learning community depend on one another.

Here are other ideas for teaching systems concepts:

- In math, science, and social studies, students can graph changes over time using methods appropriate to their age. For example, second graders might track daily temperatures on a graph template you create, while middle school or high school students can create graphs of population or migration patterns. (Note that systems modeling is a Crosscutting Concept of the Next Generation Science Standards [NGSS Lead States, 2013]).

• When studying fiction, elementary students can diagram characters' motivations, their actions, and the impacts on themselves and other characters. This can be useful in older grades as well, with the complexity of the task adjusted accordingly.

• Have students pinpoint replicating patterns ("feedback loops") in discipline-specific topics. In a high school or college unit on the Civil Rights movements, students can link causes of civil disobedience, police responses, and the impact of those responses on subsequent protests. In science (middle grades and up), topics might include population dynamics; in math, exponential growth is a common example. As with any topic, the depth of work can be scaled to students' capabilities.

• In physical education, elementary students and higher can consider the vicious cycle between, for example, team attitude and performance. If motivation is down, performance will likely suffer, further reducing motivation. The same dynamic may apply to students' individual emotional states, making systems thinking a useful way to teach the self-regulation aspects of social-emotional learning (Bateson, 2004).

Becoming Aware: Empathy, Social Consciousness, and Critical Thinking

A systems perspective makes students better thinkers, but to be effective actors, they also need to be invested in the people and places around them. This disposition of caring starts with empathy, "the act of perceiving, understanding, experiencing, and responding to the emotional state" of another person (Barker, 2003, p. 141). Compassion, a related concept, refers to concern for others and a desire to alleviate their suffering (Goetz, Keltner, & Simon-Thomas, 2010). Both empathy and compassion involve perspective-taking, the willingness and ability to view a situation through another's eyes (Todd & Galinsky, 2014). Together, these prosocial dispositions foster cooperation, altruism, and reduced stereotyping (Hoffman, 2000; Singer & Lamm, 2009). Conversely, a lack of these traits is associated with aggression, stereotyping, and scapegoating (Glick, 2008; Goleman, 1994).

Whereas empathy attunes us to the needs of individuals, *social empathy* connects us to the realities and injustices experienced by other groups (Morrell, 2010; Rifkin, 2009; Segal, 2011). Social empathy involves perspective-taking, recognizing the limitations of our own viewpoint, walking around in another's shoes, and comparing their path with our own. By dismantling the artificial walls, we become aware of connections that were always there and forge emotional ties that humanize the Other. Social empathy thus leads us to a shared understanding of our reciprocal responsibilities to one another, echoing a principle of democracy (Berman, 1997).

But learning social consciousness takes more than sharing feelings. Students must also engage in analysis and reflection, important elements of critical thinking (Curry-Stevens, 2007). This sought-after competency includes many subskills, including the ability to judge the validity of ideas or claims, form logical conclusions, recognize bias or flaws in reasoning, identify relevant information, and monitor one's thinking (Beyer, 1984, 1985; Ennis, 1962; Schroyens, 2005).

Contrary to the narrative in the Story of More—that self-interest is humans' most powerful motivator—we do have innate tendencies for prosocial behaviors. These capacities stem from a combination of hard wiring and intentional cultural practices (Bell, Richerson, & McElreath, 2009). As Segal (2011) noted, "Nature may give us the basic tools to be empathic and socially responsible, but we need social guidance to do so collectively on an ongoing basis" (p. 273). Empathy is thus a muscle we're born with—one we can develop in students or allow to atrophy. The good news is that empathy and perspective-taking can be folded into most disciplines and grades.

In early childhood education, we can foster empathy using face-to-face play, stories, and books featuring diverse people and places; exploring our similarities and differences with others; and implementing democratic classroom practices such as "circle time" (Eisenberg & Strayer, 1990). Engaging young children in acts of nurturing, such as helping to care for a pet, are other ways to fortify the empathy muscle (Wilson, 2014).

Older students also need learning experiences that call upon them to "try on" different perspectives through activities such as role plays, simulations, and reading (auto)biographies. An ongoing habit of thinking, reflecting, and comparing one's experiences with others' can help students from different backgrounds construct a shared understanding of the world (Hoffman, 2000; Morrell, 2010). Empathy thus leads us to the irrefutable truth that we're all in this together.

So how can we foster critical inquiry and perspective-taking in students? Table 6.3 identifies a set of skills and the questions that activate them (while leaving ample space for students' own questions). The section after the table provides examples of applications in different disciplines.

These questioning strategies have an obvious home in language arts, but they also apply to other disciplines. For example, in social studies, students can view events in their historical context and contrast that with contemporary ideals. A basic (if overused) example is Columbus's "discovery of America"; students could compare fifteenth-century worldviews with the perspectives of

TABLE 6.3 Inquiry Skills and Activating Questions

Inquiry skills	Questions
Raising questions	What are you wondering about? What would you like to find out?
Identifying perspectives	Whose perspective/story is this? What is the source? Can we trust it? What are different ways to look at this?
Uncovering assumptions and motivations	What do/did people know or believe about this? How did that impact their decision? What values does the decision reflect?
Identifying causes	Why do you think this happened? What influenced the event?
Identifying patterns and trends	Is this a one-time occurrence, or is there a pattern we should examine?
Comparing experiences of self and others	How do our experiences differ? What can we learn from one another? How are different [people, communities, cultures] affected?
Considering social and historical contexts	What would your life be like if you lived at that time/place; were a different race/gender/etc.? What opportunities would you have or not have?
Considering alternatives, challenging inevitability	How could have things gone differently if A, B, or C had or hadn't happened? What could change in our lives, communities, or the world based on what we do now?
Generating applications and solutions	How can we use this information in beneficial ways? What are the consequences on XYZ solution?

indigenous people then and now. By "contemplat[ing] the codes of behavior" from different timeframes (Wineburg, 2001, p. 9), students gain insights into the ways mindsets, worldviews, and conceptions of fairness evolve over time.

In STEM fields, students can interrogate statistics, research, or the uses of science. For example, a high school biology teacher framed a unit with the question, Do you own your cells? The first part of the unit focused on cell functions as mandated in the standards. To put this into a compelling context, students examined the case of Henrietta Lacks, whose cancer cells became the basis of profitable medical research without her consent. Students also evaluated stem cells research from the perspectives of a patient with a rare disease, a scientist, a biotech company, and an ethicist. The unit met multiple standards with a framing that amplified their impact.

Elementary students can also consider applications of science in age-appropriate ways. For example, in a fourth-grade class in northern Minnesota, students inventoried the invasive species in a stand of native sugar maples and worked with the local university to determine the financial impacts on the community's maple syrup producers.

Speaking and Listening Together: Equity-Literate Communication

An inclusive society depends on communicating and working with people of all backgrounds. Citizens (and that includes students) must learn how culture affects different facets of communication, such as body language, degrees of emotional disclosure, and norms of speaking and listening (Bennett, 1998). But too often, learning stays at the more superficial level of "cultural appreciation" or celebrating diversity, as addressed in Chapter 5. While valuable, this approach masks underlying power dynamics among social groups. Communication skills must therefore be informed by equity literacy, the ability to "recognize and respond justly to the insidious and often implicit" inequalities (Gorski, 2016, p. 224).

Following is a brief list of strategies for equity-literate communication (note some overlaps with the skills in Table 6.3). As you read, consider approaches you may already be using:

- Establish norms for conversations that include listening, asking clarifying questions, and speaking for one's self.
- Help students understand how their behaviors may be received and interpreted differently than intended.
- Recognize the limitations of the Golden Rule (treat others as you would want to be treated). For example, a boy who greets male friends with friendly back thumps can't assume this is appropriate for everyone. Instead, establish the Platinum Rule: Treat others the way *they* want. As a first step, students can demonstrate what respect looks and sounds like for them (eye contact? a hug? a particular greeting?). This will help students expand their repertoire of verbal and nonverbal communication skills.
- Model questions aimed at clarifying misconceptions or assumptions: Can you help me understand …. I always thought that …, but now I'm hearing ….
- Differentiate among facts, opinions, anecdotes, and verifiable patterns: What can we conclude from the evidence we have? What other information do we need?
- Have students identify the basis for their beliefs: What in your experience leads you to this conclusion?
- Help students manage responses to their personal "trigger points" (e.g., mentions of privilege).
- Acknowledge that missteps will be made. When they are, be earnest when apologizing and gracious when forgiving.
- Respond to inappropriate behavior by describing impacts (When I hear that, I feel/think/wonder …) and seeking understanding (What in your experiences leads you to say that?).

- If student A dismisses or denies student B's experiences, acknowledge A's position, but challenge A to identify the blockages: I understand this has not happened to you, but what would it mean if [this injustice] was a reality for others?

These guidelines are commonly employed to create "safe spaces" for confronting oppression. While learning environments must provide safety from physical harm, violence, or intimidation (Hardiman, Jackson, & Griffin, 2007), the fact is, learning about social justice involves emotional risks and exposure (What should I say? What am I willing to hear? What will I be asked to do or give up?). Arao and Clemens (2013) cautioned educators to not conflate "safety with comfort" (p. 135) because doing so invites knee-jerk claims of "discomfort" that hand privileged groups a convenient escape from confronting the inequitable structures they benefit from. Withdrawal by dominant individuals also closes down the discussion, silencing members of subordinate groups and inhibiting all from challenging the social arrangements. To prevent this, Arao and Clemens advocated for "brave spaces": settings where discomfort is acknowledged and embraced, and missteps are regarded as opportunities for emotional development. In a brave space, people face up to their beliefs, actions, and their impacts, intended or not. Emotional bravery thus calls us to the disquieting work of self-examination and truly listening.

This is a good opportunity to reiterate that fostering courageous communication does not mean that "anything goes." While it's our duty to create space for different viewpoints—even unpopular ones—not all speech is legally protected. Moreover, we must guide students to think through misconceptions and implications of acting on ideas. For example, if a student espouses racist views, it's our responsibility to help them uncover the source of these beliefs and question whether such ideals—and acting upon them—have a place in our democracy.

Envisioning Alternatives: Growth Mindset, Self-Efficacy, and Agency

Emeritus educator David Orr (1994) told us that learning "carries with it the responsibility to see that it is well used in the world" (p. 13). This highlights the need for students to apply their learning in ethical and effective ways. But what if students are apathetic or discouraged, trapped in story that's going nowhere—or worse, downhill? How do we help them throw off despondency and muster the optimism that they have the power to change the story? This requires cultivating another set of dispositions: growth mindset, self-efficacy, and agency.

Carol Dweck (1986, 2006) popularized the concept of *growth mindset:* the belief that one's intelligence and abilities can develop over time. In contrast, a fixed mindset regards intelligence or talents as unchangeable. Consequently, educators are encouraged to praise effort ("You really tried hard!") rather than innate capacity ("You're so smart!"). Researchers, including Dweck, have focused on the relationship between growth mindset and achievement, particularly among low-income students. For example, Claro, Paunesku, and Dweck (2016) found that (a) lower-income students are twice as likely to have a fixed mindset as their higher-income peers; and (b) growth mindset is one predictor of achievement, especially among low-income students. This builds on earlier studies showing that growth mindset can bolster motivation and resiliency (Yeager & Dweck, 2012).

But there are some big caveats. Simply praising effort alone—what Dweck (2016) referred to as a "false growth mindset" (p. 3)—can actually backfire, causing adolescents in particular to have less faith in their capacity for improvement (Amemiya & Want, 2017). Instead, educators must support students to reflect upon their thinking processes and behaviors using strategies such as those in Table 6.4. Another trap is that pinning achievement on mindset alone puts success solely on students' shoulders, isolating it from systemic factors. To their credit, Dweck and colleagues pointed out that fixating on growth mindset without attending to structural interventions "would stand at odds with decades of research and our own data" (Claro, Paunesku, & Dweck, 2016, p. 8667). They added, "To be clear, we are not suggesting that structural factors … are less important than psychological factors. Nor are we saying that teaching students a growth mindset is a substitute for systemic efforts to alleviate poverty and economic inequality" (p. 8667). In other words—as we addressed in Chapter 5—grit is not enough. Additionally, the authors pointed to the vicious cycle connecting structural and psychological factors: Consistent setbacks in the face of institutional barriers can cause a person to doubt his or her innate abilities, calcifying a fixed mindset.

In schools, this cycle is further compounded by a problem addressed in Chapter 5: low expectations. Expecting little from students sends the message that they lack innate abilities, making it unlikely that effort will even be recognized. As educator Luke Woods pointed out, praising effort is thus meaningless if teachers have yet to affirm students' abilities (Hilton, 2017). "If you come from a community where you have never received messages like that from faculty members and educators," he noted, "it's important at some point to be able to hear, you know what? You have the ability to do this" (para. 4). For Woods, growth mindset was "not wrong, but incomplete" (para. 2). Affirming students' abilities and assets can support students to believe in the potential for new possibilities. This connects to two other concepts: self-efficacy and agency.

Self-efficacy refers to confidence in one's abilities to achieve a task. *Agency* puts this into action through proactive efforts to influence one's circumstances rather than simply being "products of them" (Bandura, 1977, 2005, p. 9). These dispositions work together: Self-efficacy (belief in abilities) fuels agency (effort) given that, not surprisingly, people are more likely to persevere if they believe they can be successful (Lunenburg, 2011).

Mindsets such as optimism and hope can also nurture proactive responses to environmental stressors such as eco-anxiety, discussed in Chapter 1. For example, Ojala (2015) found that higher levels of hope were linked to stronger agency and proenvironmental behavior. This reinforcing link between human health and environmental health seen throughout the book only strengthens the case for nature exploration and outdoor play as discussed in Chapter 4 (Carmi, Arnon, & Orion, 2015).

Growth mindset, self-efficacy, and agency are broadly applicable across the curriculum. Table 6.4 offers examples of adaptable strategies.

TABLE 6.4 Strategies to Teach Growth Mindset, Self-Efficacy, and Agency

Skill	Teaching strategies
Setting short-term academic goals (e.g., for a lesson or day)	Student sets a goal (e.g., revising a document) and identifies criteria for success. The teacher helps the student monitor progress.
Planning for and believing that change is possible	Students imagine what they would like to see different, along with a time frame as appropriate, such as, "In one week, I'd like [this] to be different."
Assessing progress, identifying setbacks and progress	Students identify steps taken and evaluate the success of each. Students then reflect on reasons for the outcomes. "When I tried [this], [this] happened because …."
Revising course of action	Based on progress so far, students think of other approaches and predict what might happen. Prompts: "I tried [this] before and [this] happened. If I [try this] instead, I think [this] might happen because …."
Identifying needs and seeking support	Students articulate what they need to overcome a challenge (e.g., something material, physical, or emotional) and identify people and resources.
Developing a belief in one's ability to change and improve	Students interview a friend or family member about a time they developed a skill over a 3–6 month time frame (e.g., practicing basketball over the summer and then making the team). Students create a time line of that person's journey: What strategies did the person use? How did the person handle setbacks? Who or what supported the person? Students then develop their own plan with illustrated milestones.

Traits such as conscientiousness, thoughtfulness, and managing impulses are examples of other competencies that can contribute to student success. However, as discussed in Chapter 1, students impacted by trauma and toxic stress may exhibit just the opposite: a low threshold for frustration, impulsivity, gaps in social skills, less empathy for others, weaker communication skills, and an inability to focus or regulate emotions. Living in a heightened sense of threat, a traumatized student may interpret a pat on the back as a precursor to more abuse, triggering hyperreactivity (Shields & Cicchetti, 1998).

In response, trauma-informed practice aims to "address the consequences of trauma … and facilitate healing" to improve social and academic outcomes (National Center for Trauma-Informed Care, 2017). As with social-emotional learning strategies, trauma-informed practices have a place across grades and disciplines.

To begin, teachers can create classroom routines and structures that establish safety and building meaningful relationships. This includes giving students time, space, and opportunities to regulate emotions; develop new response techniques; and practice "mindfulness," that is, learning to relax and focus on immediate thoughts, feelings, and sensory stimulation (Carello & Butler, 2014; Conley, 2015). Multiple studies involving children and teens have pointed to the effectiveness of music therapy (Validillez, 2017), art therapy (Durhan, 2016), and physical education (Ahn & Fedewa, 2011) in improving cognitive function and reducing psychological distress. Younger students can engage in free play, arts, and drama to communicate emotions while gaining language and interpersonal skills. Older students might engage in journaling or group discussions that relate their own experiences to characters in history or literature. Regardless of the strategy, the goal is not a separate curriculum or lowered expectations, but rather "giving students the support they need to access your regular curriculum" (Flannery, 2016, para 26).

Creativity

Creativity features prominently in the 21st century skills discussion, and while the exact meaning is contested, two working definitions include "put[ting] things together in new ways" (Brookhart, 2013, para. 9) and "original and of high quality" (Perkins, 1981, p. 6). Looking beyond Western constructs, indigenous scholars, artists, and spiritual practices offer other ways to conceptualize creativity (Guntarik & Daley, 2017).

In terms of sustainability and social justice, creativity paired with agency equips students to combat problems and envision different possibilities (acknowledging that this may include traditional ideas). Students can also use creativity to demonstrate their learning in novel ways. Here are a few of my favorite examples:

- To combat harassment of immigrants in their community, fifth graders created biographies of new residents, complete with photos and oral histories. The work was displayed at the local library.

- As a culminating project in a unit on turning points in civilization, a high school student with an interest in dance created choreography to represent the agricultural revolution, the industrial revolution, and the information age. For example, forceful digging and pushing (the physical labor of planning and plowing) gave way to repetitive, mechanical movements to symbolize industrial assembly lines.
- To demonstrate their understanding of agricultural history and contemporary food security, two college freshmen created a Monopoly-style game that pulled players (representing small farmers around the world) into a vicious cycle of loans, expansion, and debt. Players escaped the trap through strategies such as forming a cooperative or reviving agricultural methods less dependent on expensive technological inputs.

These examples are not just cute entertainment that puts cleverness over learning. On the contrary, in each example, the teacher also used more conventional assessments such as papers and tests. For example, the agriculture game was accompanied by a research report and a social media campaign to promote the local farmers market. Such projects thus exemplify ways to combine differentiated instruction and multiple forms of assessments.

Chapter Takeaways

This chapter comes down to a set of tightly connected takeaways:

- Regardless of grade or discipline, we can reframe content knowledge, skills, and dispositions to help students view themselves as actors and authors capable of writing alternative narratives.
- When students understand problems and have confidence in their ability to change, they're more likely to define effective solutions, set goals, and persevere to make them happen.
- Together, the body of strategies says one clear thing students need to hear: *I believe in you.* This communicates the high expectations we know are vital to student success. Yes, students must work hard, but they also need the critical thinking skills to challenge the roadblocks that undermine their best efforts.

With a firm foundation in content and pedagogy, you're ready to take stock of the particular unit or course you plan to reframe. The Part II Culminating Activity, supported by rubrics available on the book's website, will guide you through the process. You'll then begin the roll-up-your-sleeves instructional reframing process in Part III.

References

Ahn, S., & Fedewa, A. L. (2011). A meta-analysis of the relationship between children's physical activity and mental health. *Journal of Pediatric Psychology, 36*(4), 385–397.

Amemiya, J., & Wang, M.-T. (2017). Transactional relations between motivational beliefs and help seeking from teachers and peers across adolescence. *Journal of Youth and Adolescence, 46*(8), 1743–1757.

Arao, B., & Clemens, K. (2013). From safe spaces to brave spaces: A new way to frame dialogue around diversity and social justice. In L. Landreman (Ed.), *The art of effective facilitation: Reflections from social justice educators* (pp. 135–150). Sterling, VA: Stylus.

Bandura, A. (1977). Self-efficacy: Toward a unifying theory of behavioral change. *Psychological Review, 84*(2), 191–215.

Bandura, A. (2005). The evolution of social cognitive theory. In K. G. Smith & M. A. Hitt (Eds.), *Great minds in management: The process of theory development* (pp. 9–35). New York, NY: Oxford University Press.

Barker, R. L. (2003). *The social work dictionary.* Washington, DC: NASW Press.

Bateson, M. C. (2004). *Willing to learn: Passages of personal discovery.* Hanover, NH: Steerforth Press.

Bell, A. V., Richerson, P. J., & McElreath, R. (2009). Culture rather than genes provides greater scope for the evolution of large-scale human prosociality. *Proceedings of the National Academy of Sciences, 106*(42), 17671–17674.

Bennett, M. J. (1998). *Basic concepts of intercultural communication: Selected readings.* Yarmouth, ME: Intercultural Press.

Berman, S. (1997). *Children's social consciousness and the development of social responsibility.* Albany, NY: State University of New York Press.

Beyer, B. K. (1984). Improving thinking skills: Defining the problem. *Phi Delta Kappan, 65*(7), 486–490.

Beyer, B. K. (1985). Critical thinking: What is it? *Social Education, 49*(4), 270–276.

Brookhart, S. M. (2013). Assessing creativity. *Educational Leadership, 70*(5), 28–34.

Carello, J., & Butler, L. D. (2014). Potentially perilous pedagogies: Teaching trauma is not the same as trauma-informed teaching. *Journal of Trauma & Dissociation, 15*(2), 153–168.

Carmi, N., Arnon, S., & Orion, N. (2015). Transforming environmental knowledge into behavior: The mediating role of environmental emotions. *Journal of Environmental Education, 46*(3), 183–201.

Claro, S., Paunesku, D., & Dweck, C. S. (2016). Growth mindset tempers the effects of poverty on academic achievement. *Proceedings of the National Academy of Sciences, 113*(31), 8664–8668.

Cloud, J. (2016). Education for a sustainable future: Benchmarks for individual and social learning. *Journal of Sustainability Education, 14*, 1–29.

Conley, C. (2015). SEL in higher education. In J. A. Durlak, C. E. Domitrovich, R. P. Weissberg, & T. P. Gullotta (Eds.), *Handbook of social and emotional learning: Research and practice* (pp. 197–212). New York, NY: Guilford Press.

Costanza, R. (1990). Escaping the overspecialisation trap: Creating incentives for a transdisciplinary synthesis. In M. E. Clark, & S. A. Wawrytko (Eds.), *Rethinking the curriculum: Toward an integrated interdisciplinary college education* (pp. 95–106). New York, NY: Greenwood Press.

Curry-Stevens, A. (2007). New forms of transformative education: Pedagogy for the privileged. *Journal of Transformative Education, 5*(1), 33–58.

Duncan-Andrade, J. (2007). Gangstas, wankstas, and ridas: Defining, developing, and supporting effective teachers in urban schools. *International Journal of Qualitative Studies in Education, 20*(6), 617–638.

Durham, H. (2016, December 13). How art can help children overcome trauma. *Education Week.*

Dweck, C. S. (1986). Motivational processes affecting learning. *American Psychologist, 41*(10), 1040–1048.

Dweck, C. S. (2006). *Mindset: The new psychology of success.* New York, NY: Random House.

Dweck, C. S. (2016, January 13). What having a "growth mindset" actually means [Web log post]. *Harvard Business Review.*

Eisenberg, N., & Strayer, J. (Eds.). (1990). *Empathy and its development.* New York, NY: Cambridge University Press.

Ennis, R. H. (1962). A concept of critical thinking. *Harvard Educational Review, 32*(1), 81–111.

Flannery, M. (2016). *Growth mindset and its impact on learning and school culture* [Sabbatical report]. Retrieved from https://jessicatalbot.net/growth-mindset-powerpoint.html

Glick, P. (2008). When neighbors blame neighbors: Scapegoating and the breakdown of ethnic relations. In V. M. Esses, & R. A. Vernon (Eds.), *Explaining the breakdown of ethnic relations: Why neighbors kill* (pp. 123–146). Malden, MA: Blackwell.

Goetz, J. L., Keltner, D., & Simon-Thomas, E. (2010). Compassion: An evolutionary analysis and empirical review. *Psychological Bulletin, 136*(3), 351–374. doi:10.1037/a0018807

Goleman, D. (1994). *Emotional intelligence: Why it can matter more than IQ.* New York, NY: Bantam Books.

Gorski, P. (2016). Rethinking the role of "culture" in educational equity: From cultural competence to equity literacy. *Multicultural Perspectives, 18*(4), 221–226.

Guntarik, O., & Daley, L. (2017). Indigenous creative practice research: Between convention and creativity. *New Writing, 14*(3), 409–422.

Hardiman, R., Jackson, B., & Griffin, P. (2007). Conceptual foundations for social justice education. In M. Adams, L. A. Bell, & P. Griffin (Eds.), *Teaching for diversity and social justice* (pp. 35–66). New York, NY: Routledge.

Hilton, A. A. (2017, November 12). Prominent scholar calls growth mindset a "cancerous" idea, in isolation. *Huffington Post.* Retrieved from https://www.huffingtonpost.com/entry/prominent-scholar-calls-growth-mindset-a-cancerous_us_5a07f046e4b0f1dc729a6bc3

Hoffman, M. L. (2000). *Empathy and moral development: Implications for caring and justice.* London, UK: Cambridge University Press.

Lunenburg, F. C. (2011). Self-efficacy in the workplace: Implications for motivation and performance. *International Journal of Management, Business, and Administration, 14*(1), 1–6.

Meadows, D. H. (2008). *Thinking in systems: A primer.* White River Junction, VT: Chelsea Green.

Morrell, M. E. (2010). *Empathy and democracy: Feeling, thinking, and deliberation.* University Park, PA: Pennsylvania State University Press.

National Center for Trauma-Informed Care. (2017). *Trauma-informed approach.* Retrieved from https://www.samhsa.gov/nctic

NGSS Lead States. (2013). *Next Generation Science Standards: For states, by states. Three dimensional learning.* Retrieved from https://www.nextgenscience.org/three-dimensions

Nolet, V. (2013). Teacher education and ESD in the United States: The vision, challenges, and implementation. In R. McKeown, & V. Nolet (Eds.), *Schooling for sustainable development in Canada and the United States* (pp. 53–67). New York, NY: Springer.

Ojala, M. (2015). Hope in the face of climate change: Associations with environmental engagement and student perceptions of teachers' emotion communication style and future orientation. *Journal of Environmental Education, 46*(3), 133–148.

Orr, D. (1994). *Earth in mind: On education, environment, and the human prospect.* Washington, DC: Island Press.

Perkins, D. N. (1981). *The mind's best work.* Cambridge, MA: Harvard University Press.

Rifkin, J. (2009). *The empathic civilization: The race to global consciousness in a world in crisis.* New York, NY: Penguin Books.

Schroyens, W. (2005). Review of the book *Knowledge and thought: An introduction to critical thinking,* by D. Halpern. *Experimental Psychology, 52*(2), 163–164.

Segal, E. A. (2011). Social empathy: A model built on empathy, contextual understanding, and social responsibility that promotes social justice. *Journal of Social Service Research, 37*(3), 266–277.

Shields, A., & Cicchetti, D. (1998). Reactive aggression among maltreated children: The contributions of attention and emotion dysregulation. *Journal of Clinical Child Psychology, 27*(4), 381–395.

Singer, T., & Lamm, C. (2009). The social neuroscience of empathy. *Annals of the New York Academy of Sciences, 1156*(1), 81–96.

Sipos, Y. (2009). Non-traditional pedagogies in advanced education: Engaging head, hands and heart for environmental and educational benefit. In S. Allen-Gil, L, Stelljes, & O. Borysova (Eds.), *Addressing global environmental security through innovative educational curricula* (pp. 155–164). Dordrecht, Netherlands: Springer.

Sweeney, L. B., & Meadows, D. (2010). *The systems thinking playbook: Exercises to stretch and build learning and systems thinking capabilities.* White River Junction, VT: Chelsea Green.

Todd, A. R., & Galinsky, A. D. (2014). Perspective-taking as a strategy for improving intergroup relations: Evidence, mechanisms, and qualifications. *Social and Personality Psychology Compass, 8*(7), 374–387.

Valdillez, K. (2017, March 1). Music therapy offers healing to Tulalip–Marysville community. *Tulalip News.*

Wickson, F., Carew, A. L., & Russell, A. W. (2006, November). Transdisciplinary research: Characteristics, quandaries and quality. *Futures, 38*(9), 1046–1059.

Wilson, R. (2014, December 23). Caring for plants and animals fosters empathy. *Teaching Tolerance.* Retrieved from https://www.tolerance.org/magazine/caring-for-plants-and-animals-fosters-empathy

Wineburg, S. (2001). *Historical thinking and other unnatural acts: Charting the future of teaching the past.* Philadelphia, PA: Temple University Press.

Yeager, D. S., & Dweck, C. S. (2012). Mindsets that promote resilience: When students believe that personal characteristics can be developed. *Educational Psychologist, 47*(4), 302–314.

PART II

Culminating Activity
Curriculum Self-Assessment

Chapters 4–6 introduced philosophies and practices to guide our curriculum, as well as ones to avoid. Your next steps are to (a) identify a unit or course to reframe in Part III, and (b) identify existing strengths and areas to adapt. For this activity, you will turn to the book's website, where you'll find rubrics to guide you through this process. These rubrics integrate the competencies and instructional approaches we've covered so far, focusing on the broad strokes of content and pedagogy.

Before you access the rubrics, select the unit or course you want to reframe, and gather related artifacts such as syllabi, unit and lesson plans, instructional resources, assessment tools, and student work. A wide range of materials will enable you to conduct a more thorough assessment. You'll find further directions on the website.

PART III

Changing the Story

Curriculum Design with the Stakes in Mind

The moment has finally arrived: It's time to (re)design the unit, course, or module you've selected (we'll use those three terms somewhat interchangeably). Whether you're creating a curriculum makeover or designing something from scratch, you'll reframe the content and pedagogy in ways that meet your required outcomes while also infusing the principles of sustainability and social justice. Part III (Chapters 7–10) will lead you through a stepwise process to get there.

We've used the story metaphor through this book, and it's an apt framing as you step into the role of curriculum author. Moreover, your completed work will unfold like a compelling narrative—one that anchors students in a meaningful plot, guides them through critical inquiry, and challenges them to craft a positive resolution. The arc of inquiry will develop over three clear phases:

Stage 1. The story begins: Your opening lessons will introduce central topics (the plot), people (actors), and places (setting). Students will discover how the plot relates to their lives and communities, raise their own questions, and come to see themselves among the actors with a stake in the outcome.

Stage 2. The plot thickens: Students deepen the investigations through ongoing, critical inquiry. Along the way, they will acquire the knowledge and competencies needed to take action and change the narrative. This is the heart of the unit.

Stage 3. Decision-making and action: The story reaches the climax, putting learners in the role of empowered authors who must determine the ending. Students will assess solutions, make ethical decisions, and develop a solution-oriented project that wraps up the current story or sets the stage for a whole new learning adventure.

Figure III.1 illustrates the framework.

To develop your unit or course, you'll complete a series of distinct design steps, one per chapter as follows. Each step applies to the entire unit.

FIGURE III.1 Unit or Course Progression.

- Chapter 7: "Defining the Plot"
- Chapter 8: "Creating Intrigue and Suspense With Guiding Questions"
- Chapter 9: "Defining and Sequencing the Learning Outcomes"
- Chapter 10: "Aligning Outcomes, Standards, Instruction, and Assessment"

Again, at each step, you'll be designing for unit or course as a whole. The result will be a coherent narrative rather than a collection of isolated lessons.

Note that the process includes elements you may be familiar with, such as learning outcomes and aligning standards. But there are also some new dimensions, including the positioning of the standards within the unit; this is addressed in Chapters 9 and 10.

Just as stories come in all sizes—from trilogies to novels to short stories—so do units and courses. Thus, you'll have to consider the overall length of instruction and how you'll allocate time among topics or lessons. We'll revisit these considerations throughout the design process.

In terms of actual instructional resources, start with your existing materials, given the process is essentially a curriculum makeover. As your work progresses, you'll probably come up with ideas for adaptations and/or identify new resources. Regardless, approach this process with a spirit of flexibility and creativity.

The following tools offer additional support:

- An editable Curriculum Design Template is available on the book's website. You'll record your work here (or on a hard copy). The completed document will serve as your internal unit plan or syllabus blueprint. Excerpts of this template with filled-in examples appear throughout the chapters.
- Also online is a fully developed, transdisciplinary module designed with the process you're about to use. We'll reference it as we work. While this is a middle-grade unit, it was selected because the topic is relatable, meaning that you'll be able to focus on design elements or envision adaptations without unfamiliar content getting in the way.
- We'll also return to some of the tables from Chapter 6.

Gather your tools and let's get started with our first step in Chapter 7: defining a plot to serve as the focus of your unit.

7
DEFINING THE PLOT

A plot is the central problem, dilemma, or conflict of a story, and to be compelling, the characters must have something at stake, that is, something to gain or lose. The higher the stakes, the more invested we are in the outcome. Likewise, to become engaged in your unit, students need to understand what's at stake with the topic at hand. Only by understanding the consequences of action or inaction will students be able to chart a course toward the desired outcome.

In this chapter, you'll use a special method to derive a meaningful plot from the topics in your unit or course. After a brief overview, you'll walk through the method using examples from other teachers. You'll then complete the step yourself and evaluate your work using reflective questions. The outcome will be a title and a concise "blurb" you can enter into the Curriculum Design Template.

Get Started

In Chapter 6, we introduced two ways to integrate sustainability and social justice into curriculum: (a) teaching clearly related topics, such as with the online water unit; or (b) reframing *any* topic with one or more of the foundational concepts of sustainability and social justice: beauty, change, community, diversity, ecological health, equity, ethics, interdependence, limits/scale, resilience, systems, and well-being.

Look back now at Table 6.2 in Chapter 6 (pp. 113–114), which lists each concept and its applicability across disciplines. As discussed in Chapter 6, the foundational concepts infuse topics with meaning and significance—in other words, a plot with something at stake.

This is the method we're going to use in this chapter. Even if your content is already clearly related to sustainability, you'll still work with the Foundational

Concepts to ensure you have defined the stakes. For example, climate change—an obvious sustainability plot—can be taught in academic ways that are removed from the real world. But infusing the concepts of community and equity yields "plot seeds" from which more significant topics emerge, such as environmental justice and community resiliency. Overall, when we find ourselves asking, *What will happen if …?* or *What if we were able to …?*, we know we have a high-stakes plot.

See What Other Teachers Have Done

Let's look at two examples of how other teachers used the foundational concepts to surface a plot. The first concerns a high school teacher and her required unit on Ancient Civilizations. She's thinking, "What could be less relevant to my students than the aqueducts of Ancient Rome?" To reframe the topic, the teacher selects the concepts *ecological sustainability* and *community*. She organizes her ideas using Table 7.1 (excerpted from the online Curriculum Design Template).

In the left column, the teacher (like you will do) enters the selected concepts. Along the top, she enters required topics and skills. Then she writes the resulting plot ideas in the appropriate cells. Table 7.2 shows the results of the exercise.

TABLE 7.1 Applying Concepts to Topics

Concept	Topic/skill	Topic/skill	Topic/skill

TABLE 7.2 Plot Seeds for Ancient Civilizations + Ecological Sustainability + Community

Concept	Topic: Geographic factors affecting civilizations	Topic: Ancient Rome	Topic: Ancient Egypt
Ecological sustainability	Human-environmental interactions in development of civilizations: sustainable or not?	Deforestation to provide fuel for growing industries	Drought in Egypt and the impacts on irrigating from the Nile
Community	The role of our local river in the community's development: sustainable or not?	Loss of green space for new businesses in the community; green space preservation	Same

The topic/concept integration gives rise to a relevant plot with local concerns at stake. From here, the teacher develops a complete, 3-week unit called "Learning From the Past to Prepare for the Future." Here's a brief description to help you visualize how the plot seeds "sprout" into extended instruction:

> After learning about the factors affecting the development of civilizations, students will analyze the environmental, cultural, and economic issues that influenced the success or collapse of Ancient Rome and Ancient Egypt. Students will then investigate the environmental and economic changes facing their own region.

This is the type of blurb you'll write by the end of the chapter.

As another example, let's consider a middle school math teacher in a high-poverty district who is grappling with a unit on ratios. Again, the teacher wants to wrap a plot around this. He considers the fact that many local families live day-to-day and purchase individual servings of food rather than buying larger quantities, which are cheaper per unit. Building on this context, the teacher uses Table 7.1 to infuse the concepts of *equity* and *community* into his math. Table 7.3 shows his results.

The reframed unit, "Calculating Family Finances," will guide students to investigate and find solutions to the financial challenge described. In one lesson, students will use ratios, division, and other skills to compare the price of everyday foods based on volume and quantity (e.g., the cost of a pint vs. a gallon of milk). As students will discover, it's cheaper ounce-per-ounce to buy larger quantities. However, like the teacher, the students also know that some families (perhaps their own) can't afford the bigger size up front. To shift the plot in a positive direction, students might consult with a community organization to help families pool resources and organize bulk purchases.

These examples show how overlaying the right concepts can give topics a sustainability and social justice orientation. For more examples, review the sample unit online. What embedded concepts do you see? What is the plot?

TABLE 7.3 Plot Seeds for Math + Equity + Community

Concept	Topic/skill: Ratios and division	Topic/skill: Graphing	Topic/skill: Applying math in real-world contexts
Equity	Calculating per unit food prices based on quantity/volume	Graphing a family's cash flow to determine available income	Families pooling money for bulk purchases
Community	Students visiting local stores to compare prices	Graphing average household incomes	Same

One final consideration before you apply the method is the developmental readiness of your students. Young children should not be burdened with "saving the planet." Rather, content and projects in the early grades should be local and immediate, and expand as students grow older. For example, kindergarten and first-grade students might focus on questions relevant to the classroom or schoolyard. Second and third graders can address community-level concerns, and older students can engage with issues from the regional to the international levels. That said, even students in early grades should understand that the people, events, and environment they are familiar with extend beyond them in terms of both time and place. For additional ideas, please refer to the "Supplemental Resource for Chapter 6: Scaffolding Social Justice and Sustainability Topics Across Grade Bands" on the book's website.

Try It

These steps will guide you through the process:

1. Access the Curriculum Design Template online and find the online version of Table 7.1. You will enter your responses here.
2. Choose two to three of the foundational concepts that seem most relevant to your unit or course. Enter those in the left-hand column of the template (or a hard copy you recreate).
3. In the top row of the template, enter two to three specific topics or skills you need to cover.
4. Connect each concept with the topics/skills and write the resulting plot seeds in the appropriate cells. Keep your ideas loose; there's no right or wrong way to word them.
5. Based on your responses, write up a short description of what the unit will address. You don't need to describe all of the activities.

Evaluate Your Work

Use these questions to assess the strength of your reframed content (your plot):

- Does the plot address something of personal or social significance?
- Is the content developmentally appropriate?
- Does the framing invite students to consider what's at stake?
- Are there subplots to explore and connect?
- Is there a worthy challenge with possibilities for solutions?
- Can you adequately investigate the topic in the time allocated for instruction?

What Do I Share With My Students?

The outcome of this step is a unit title and blurb such as those in the examples. You can enter this information into the template and even work the language into your course description in ways that define the focus, yet don't give much away. Write a teaser for students, but hold back the full plot.

With this step completed, you're ready to open doorways into the inquiry by creating guiding questions, the focus of Chapter 8.

8

CREATING INTRIGUE AND SUSPENSE WITH GUIDING QUESTIONS

The plot you defined in Chapter 7 provides a focus for your unit or course. But how will you bring students into the learning? That is the job of guiding questions, the focus of this chapter.

Guiding questions are an instructional design element that provides entry points into the curriculum, inviting learners to uncover "the important ideas at the heart of each subject" (Wiggins & McTighe, 1998, p. 28). To create your questions, you'll first review several design factors, including question types, sequencing, and scale. Next, you'll consider the role of student-developed questions. Finally, you'll develop your own questions and assess them with a simple checklist.

Get Started

You're probably familiar with the difference between closed- and open-ended questions; the former have a single answer, whereas the latter require explanation. But both types are needed. As shown in Table 8.1, students must know the factual answer to the closed-ended question on the left before they can tackle the open-ended "What's at stake?" question on the right.

In short, students can't analyze problems without the underlying facts, meaning you'll want to develop both question types for the beginning, middle, and end of your unit depending on what students need at that moment. Do students need foundational facts? If so, turn to comprehension questions. Are students ready for analysis? Then select open-ended questions. Throughout the unit, you want students to move from acquiring facts to developing meaning.

Table 8.2 provides an overview of the role questions play at different stages of inquiry.

TABLE 8.1 Closed- and Open-Ended Questions

What are the facts? (closed-ended)	*What's at stake? (open-ended)*
How is land used in this region? What does a planning board do?	What are the social and ecological impacts of land-use decisions? How are planning decisions affecting the health of my community?

TABLE 8.2 Questions at Each Stage of a Unit: Functions and Examples

	The story begins	*The plot thickens*	*Cliffhanger/resolution*
Sample question functions	Introduce what's at stake, situate students in the inquiry, activate prior knowledge, provide *foreshadowing.*	Deepen inquiry and analysis of *subplots.*	Invite students to consider solutions, apply learning, communicate findings, and identify what's next.
Sample questions	What do we know about …? Have you ever [seen/ done/been affected by] …? What facts do we need to get to the bottom of this?	Why is this happening? What additional facts do we need? What's really going on here?	What could change based on how we steer the plot? What happens if we try …? What facts must we consider?

The table also reveals that students will need to use different cognitive levels and processes, such as recall, understand, analyze, evaluate, and apply (Bloom, 1956). Each level plays a role in students' learning journey, and well-worded questions can spark the respective cognitive processes. Further resources and sample questions for each level are available on the book's website.

One final consideration is the need to right-size questions to instructional time. For example, "What is the meaning of life?" could take a lifetime to answer. It's too big for a unit; however, you could shrink the grain size by asking, "What do the XYZ cultures/philosophies/religions say about the meaning of life?" It's still a big question, but now it has some parameters.

Consider Student-Developed Questions

Because students are *characters* experiencing the story as well as the authors crafting it, they need opportunities to raise their own questions. Great—so why not let students raise all of the questions? While completely open-ended learning can be exciting, it also presents several challenges.

First, students don't know what they don't know, meaning they may never come to pose a question about a topic they don't realize exists. (This is true for all of us.) For example, freshmen high school students shared that zoning was the most interesting topic in their exploration of land use. Why? Because students discovered that zoning influences their transportation options and thus their social lives. Relying on parents for rides—typical in residential-only neighborhoods—puts a crimp on meeting up with friends, compared to the options in a mixed-use, walkable community. This insight sparked many student questions, but it wouldn't have happened unless the teacher had provided *foreshadowing* by asking, "How do you get around? Why is your community laid out the way it is?"

The second caveat about completely student-driven units is that they can be unstructured to the point of inhibiting learning—while also leaving the teacher scrambling to find resources. For example, in a middle school class, students generated a question about energy sources (solar, etc.). Students spent a week Googling for information. But developing answers required a foundation of scientific knowledge that the teacher simply didn't provide out of a well-intentioned desire to keep the learning *student-centered*. This actually undercut learning. For example, answering a question about the efficiency of wind power required knowledge of physics. The teacher provided no instruction on this, and the student's research yielded incomplete, technical details he didn't understand.

Your goal is to balance questions you create with those students pose. Guiding questions are there to provide a framework, and this does not preclude opportunities for students to steer learning in a different direction, again supported by you. Base your decisions on students' learning needs and developmental readiness.

Let's Try It

You're now ready to develop the questions for your unit or course. Table 8.3 provides a structure to generate initial ideas. (Note that the presentation of closed-ended before open-ended questions in the table does not imply that you must use this order.) The table is simply a workspace; you'll transfer your final questions into the Curriculum Design Template.

1. Start by developing up to three overarching questions to define the parameters of instruction, considering overall time. These big questions should prompt students to consider what's at stake at the personal and/or community levels.
2. Create additional, smaller open- and closed-ended questions for each stage of the inquiry.
3. As appropriate to your instruction, earmark specific questions for each individual lessons or course session.
4. Review your work, make any changes, and transfer the final questions into the Curriculum Design Template.

TABLE 8.3 Question-Writing Structure

	Overarching questions		
	Stage 1: The story begins	Stage 2: The plot thickens	Stage 3: Resolution
Facts (closed-ended)			
Stakes (open-ended)			

Evaluate Your Work

As an informal assessment, ask yourself, *To what extent do my questions …*

- Situate students in the plot?
- Create intrigue?
- Invite investigations of subplots?
- Require that learners make connections among issues and ideas?
- Address different cognitive levels?
- Require learners to consider values and ethics?
- Encourage learners to plan and execute meaningful projects?

What Do I Give My Students?

Share your questions with students in ways that will support their learning journey. Here are some ideas:

- Include your overarching questions on the syllabus or keep them written on the board. These will serve as a road map you can refer back to throughout instruction.
- Introduce one or more smaller questions for each lesson or course session.
- Have students write the day's question in a journal at the beginning of class and use it as the basis of reflection and informal assessment.

You've done it! You've mapped out the flow of instruction, and now you're ready to define the specific learning outcomes that arise from your questions. That's the focus of Chapter 9, coming right up.

References

Bloom, B. S. (1956). *Taxonomy of educational objectives. Handbook I: The cognitive domain.* New York, NY: Longman.

Wiggins, G., & McTighe, J. (1998). *Understanding by design.* Alexandria, VA: Association for Supervision and Curriculum Development.

9

DEFINING AND SEQUENCING THE LEARNING OUTCOMES

You're making great progress: You have a high-stakes plot and a set of questions to guide the narrative. Now you're ready to define the lesson-by-lesson progression—the learning outcomes for each "chapter" of the narrative. That's what we'll focus on here.

We'll start by comparing different ways to phrase outcomes and how this influences instruction. After landing on a particular style, you'll revisit design considerations from Chapter 8 to ensure your learning outcomes are consistent with your guiding questions. With this foundation, you'll then write and sequence your outcomes.

Get Started

When you hear "learning outcome," you're probably thinking about standards, objectives, performance indicators, or related terms. So at this very moment, you may be reaching for that binder of standards or pulling up your objectives online.

Stop.

Yes, that's right. Put the binder aside and close your computer. You will not select a handful of standards or objectives, and then design a corresponding lesson for each. (Gasp.) Nor will you phrase your outcomes using the stem, *Students will be able to* (identify, describe, etc.). This, too, may be heresy; standards typically start with this stem, after all, and the phrasing yields a specific, assessable action. So why abandon these verb-based outcomes?

Fear not; you're not tossing them out. Rather, you're going to reposition when and how you use them. Your standards or other verb-based objectives will be front and center in the next chapter, but right now, we're going to learn a specific formula for writing outcomes that will ultimately strengthen your unit or course. Let's start by comparing four familiar stems:

a.   Learners will *understand* ...
b.   Learners will *understand how/why/when, etc.* ...
c.   Learners will *understand that* ...
d.   Learners *will be able to* ...

Next, take a look at examples of learning outcomes generated by each stem. The production of French fries (addressed in Chapter 3) will serve as our topic.

a.   Learners will understand the production of French fries.
b.   Learners will understand how French fries are made.
c.   Learners will understand that making French fries is a multistep process requiring energy and natural resources, while also producing wastes.
d.   Learners will be able to identify the steps involved in making French fries.

At first glance, the outcomes appear essentially the same. But the wording of each statement is instrumental in determining the scope of learning. To illustrate the differences, review the learning outcomes again and answer the questions that follow. The questions, answers, and explanations appear in Table 9.1. Don't peek!

1.   Which statement is the least specific?
2.   Which statement provides the next level of specificity?
3.   Which statement articulates a specific and assessable behavior?
4.   Which statement most clearly articulates the substance of the topic (the plot) and the underlying stakes?

Now check your responses.

TABLE 9.1 Questions, Answers, and Explanations

Questions	Responses and explanations
1. Which outcome is the least specific?	Statement a: *Learners will* **understand** *the production of* **French fries.** This statement tells us the topic, but nothing else. What does it mean to "understand"? What are the indicators? The meaning is too broad to serve as a learning outcome.
2. Which outcome provides the next level of specificity?	Statement b: *Learners will understand* **how French fries are made.** This outcomes provides more focus, but we're still left asking some questions: How exactly are French fries made? What steps do we need to know—and why does it even matter? If we haven't answered these questions in our role as the teacher, how can we expect our students to? The statement, while stronger than statement a, is still too vague to serve as a learning outcome.

(Continued)

Questions	Responses and explanations
3. Which outcome articulates a specific and assessable behavior?	Statement d: *Learners will be able to **identify the steps involved in making French fries.*** This is the type of verb-based outcome we just discussed: a clear and assessable action that indicates understanding. For example, students could identify the steps through a writing assignment. But even then, we're left wondering why it matters. Who cares how French fries are made? Unless we can answer this, identifying the steps is simply an isolated task.
4. Which statement most clearly articulates the substance of the topic and the underlying stakes?	Statement c: *Learners will understand **that making French fries is a multistep process that requires energy and natural resources, while also producing wastes.*** At last! This is what we really want students to know: the actual story of French fries. This outcome defines a clear takeaway for a specific piece of the plot. The statement also gives us a taste of what's at stake: environmental implications. Now we know why the topic matters.

This exercise shows that the stem *Students will understand that* … yields a clear principle essential to the topic (Banks, 1997; Erickson, 2007; Taba, 1967). The word *that* sets you up to write a focused takeaway. We'll also refer to these takeaways as "plot lines" because they demarcate the narrative. Note that in the Next Generation Science Standards, "that" statements are the equivalent of Disciplinary Core Ideas.

So far, so good. But how do we know students understand the learning outcome? How can we assess it? This is where we need statement d, the type of verb-based indicator we find in standards or objectives. If students can identify steps involved in making French fries, we know they understand the plot line. Statements c and d thus need each other. On its own, outcome c is vital information, but it doesn't specify an assessable behavior. Likewise, outcome d alone is merely a task without context. The task takes on significance only when it's aligned with the plot line.

This approach puts meaningful content first and positions standards as indicators that serve the larger story. Right now, we'll stay focused on generating learning outcomes; in the next chapter, you'll align those with your standards/ objectives, activities, and assessments.

If you teach a mostly skills-based subject such as math, you may be wondering whether or how this approach applies. In this case, *that* statements illuminate the principles behind the skills as well as their application. For example, a statistics teacher generated these plot lines: "Statistics is a branch of math that can help us understand [this pattern/trend in our community/the world]," and "We can use statistics to learn more about [this problem]." The instructor taught the standards, but the plot lines couched them in a purpose.

The nuances of writing outcomes for any discipline will become clearer as we examine our next step.

Consider Design Factors

Recall that in Chapter 8, you developed both closed- and open-ended questions. The former generate facts; the latter surface the stake. Likewise, you'll develop two types of learning outcomes:

- "Just the facts" outcomes define essential information, that is, the who, what, where, and when. Example: Humans rely on renewable and nonrenewable resources.
- "What's at stake" outcomes describe the consequences and significance of the facts. Example: Using renewable resources faster than they can regenerate leads to depletion.

As we've learned, facts are necessary to understand the stakes. If students don't know the information in the first statement, the consequences described in the second statement are irrelevant. You may also find that some outcomes incorporate facts and stakes, such as French fries statement c, which provides important factual information but also hints at the stakes.

Chapter 8 also introduced the importance of scaling questions to the scope and length of your unit or course. The same applies for learning outcomes; instructional time will influence the level of detail and grain size. For example, an outcome for a 30-minute activity will be smaller in scope than one for a 90-minute session. Thus, think of each plot line as an accordion that can expand or contract. For example, French fries statement c could be expanded this way: *Students will understand that growing the potato requires fertilizer and irrigation, and that harvesting the potato for French fries requires fossil fuels.* The instructor would then plan one or more lessons around each statement. Conversely, you could compress statement c into a single lesson to give the broad strokes of the topic.

Our final consideration is sequencing, also addressed in Chapter 8. You can generate a collection of exciting and well-scaled plot lines, but unless they are logically sequenced, students will stumble through the story. This means you must articulate outcomes for the beginning, middle, and end of the narrative. Here are a few guidelines:

- Plot lines at the beginning of a unit will introduce the plot and establish its relevance. For example, a chemistry instructor might begin a unit with plot lines such as "We use chemicals in our everyday lives" and "Chemistry impacts the health of our water."

- Plot lines in the middle of the unit will articulate more depth and complexity. For the chemistry course, outcomes may include, "Excessive exposure to lead causes health problems."
- Plot lines that wrap up the unit will focus on solutions and actions. Examples might include "Ways to solve [this problem] include X, Y, Z," or "Solution X will impact [this group in this way]."

Let's Try It

It's time to write your outcomes using our "that" formula. I recommend that you write individual statements on sticky notes so that you can move them as your sequence takes form. You can then transfer your final ideas into the Curriculum Design Template. Here are suggested steps:

1. First, review your guiding questions and write "answers" (to the extent you can) using *that* statements. You don't need to write one outcome for each question; however, you should reference the questions to ensure the unit's or course's elements are consistent.
2. Write outcomes that define the takeaway(s) for each activity, lesson, or course session. Be sure to consider both the facts and the stakes.
3. Match grain size to allocated instructional time. How much detail can/do you want to go into? How specific should each statement be?
4. Allow time and flexibility in your unit for student-driven shifts in inquiry.

Evaluate Your Work

Use the criteria in Table 9.2 to assess your outcomes.

Do I Share the Outcomes With My Students?

Generally speaking, the outcomes represent the AHA insights you want students to figure out through the inquiry; telling students the information gives away the story. However, much depends on the type of instructional strategy you're using and where it falls on the spectrum of direct instruction (e.g., a lecture) and constructivist learning, which engages learners in exploration and discovery.

Coming up in Chapter 10, you'll align learning outcomes, standards, activities, and assessments. It's the final step of the process. Ready to go?

TABLE 9.2 Criteria for Assessing Learning Outcomes

My learning outcomes …	Not yet	I'm getting there	I'm there
Provide bridges to learners' lives, cultures, and communities.			
Define both the facts and the stakes of the investigation.			
Build the knowledge base students need to steer the narrative toward a positive ending.			
Integrate social, environmental, economic, political, and cultural dimensions as applicable.			
Encourage connections across time, place, and scale (thinking in systems).			
Probe students to consider issues from different perspectives.			
Guide students to make informed decisions and develop a culminating project.			

References

Banks, J. A. (1997). *Educating citizens in a multicultural society.* New York, NY: Teachers College Press.

Erickson, H. L. (2007). *Stirring the head, heart, and soul: Redefining curriculum, instruction, and concept-based learning.* Thousand Oaks, CA: Corwin Press.

Taba, H. (1967). *Teachers' handbook for elementary social studies.* Palo Alto, CA: Addison-Wesley.

10

ALIGNING OUTCOMES, STANDARDS, INSTRUCTION, AND ASSESSMENT

In the last chapter you defined the learning outcomes/plot lines for your unit or course phrased as, *Students will understand that*. Putting the standards aside for that step may have left you uncomfortable, but this chapter will put them front and center. In the coming pages, you'll embed your standards or other objectives into your unit, and then align them with activities and assessments. Again, you'll use the Curriculum Design Template. This is the final step, so let's get started.

Embed Your Standards

As we've discussed, standards and other verb-based objectives play a unique role in this design method, which puts the narrative first. Thus, rather than being ends in themselves, standards support the plot by defining the assessable behaviors that tell us whether students have mastered them. This approach ensures standards are taught in a meaningful context. Let's look at two examples.

As shown in the right-hand column of Table 10.1, our first standard addresses cell division.

Note that this standard already has some built-in content, making it very clear. However, as written, we really don't know why the standard matters—that is, until we position it next to the plot line (regarding cancer) in the left-hand column. The standard thus defines a skill students need to understand cancer.

Unlike the science standard example, many standards (including Common Core) do not specify any content, but rather emphasize skills. This provides a golden opportunity to put the standards in a meaningful context. Consider the examples in Table 10.2. The left side shows examples of learning outcomes for a plot about food systems. In the right column, you'll see a standard presented

TABLE 10.1   Comparing Plot Lines and Standards

Plot Line	Standard
Cell division is a process that is regulated and, when left unchecked, cancer results.	Explain how cell division is regulated and the repercussions that result when the cell division process is not regulated.

two ways: (a) as written, and (b) with the plot embedded. The first row provides a language arts example; the second row, math.

Putting aside Common Core's larger controversies, including its deafening silence on democracy (Wraga, 2010, para. 9), the examples show that these content-neutral standards provide a strong platform for teaching sustainability and social justice. Indeed, when you have a compelling plot, you'll likely meet more standards than ever because the worthy challenges require that students acquire an integrated set of skills. Learning thus becomes more impactful by foregrounding the narrative.

TABLE 10.2   Putting Standards in Context

Learning outcomes/plot lines: Students will understand that …	Standard presented two ways
Food traditions vary by person, family, culture, and community.	a. Language Arts Anchor Standard for Reading as written (CCRA.R.7): Integrate and evaluate content presented in diverse media and formats, including visually and quantitatively, as well as in words. b. The same standard with *plot embedded:* Integrate and evaluate content about *food traditions* presented in diverse media and formats, including visually and quantitatively, as well as in words, *such as family photos, interviews, folktales, and data compiled from these.*
The availability of fresh and healthy food varies by community. Uneven access can contribute to health problems.	a. Math Ratios and Proportional Relationships standard as written (7.RP.A): Analyze proportional relationships and use them to solve real-world mathematical problems. b. The same standard with *plot embedded:* Analyze proportional relationships *about demographics and food access, such as the number of stores per X square miles,* and use [the relationships] to solve real-world mathematical *and community* problems.

Align Learning Activities and Assessments

Standards need activities to come to life, and this highlights the other benefit of this method: activity options. For example, the rewritten language arts standard automatically suggests ideas such as conducting interviews.

Let's expand on this in Table 10.3. It reproduces the first row of Table 10.2 and adds a third column for activities.

Here, activities such as creating oral histories and a guidebook of food traditions are authentic ways to bring the standard to life. In terms of activity types for your discipline, you can employ a range of strategies you are already using. Assessments, which are also in the third column, are measures of student learning used to make instructional decisions (Wiggins & McTighe, 2005). This can include preassessments before instruction, summative assessments after instruction, and formative assessments that gather data during instruction to help guide it (Brookhart, 2011). Combining activities and assessments is intentional to emphasize that assessment and learning activities inform each other.

Regardless of the type, a strong assessment has these traits (Wiggins & McTighe, 2005):

- Establishes a clear goal;
- Defines criteria for acceptable evidence of mastery;
- Requires students to make their learning visible;
- Drives instructional decisions; and
- Engages learners in monitoring their own learning.

There are more assessment strategies than we could ever cover here, and assessments will, of course, vary by grade level and discipline.

TABLE 10.3 Aligned Plot Line, Standard, and Activities/Assessments

Learning outcomes/ plot lines	Standard (with plot embedded)	Activities/assessments
Food traditions vary by person, family, culture, and community.	Integrate and evaluate content about *food traditions* presented in diverse media and formats, including visually and quantitatively, as well as in words, *such as family photos, interviews, folktales, and data compiled from these.*	Conduct oral histories about family food traditions. Create a guidebook of community food traditions using primary-source information. Assess these activities with a rubric. Criteria include accurate evaluations of media and accuracy. (You can also add resources here.)

Try It

Let's pull it all together with the steps that follow. The time you need to complete them will depend on how far you've already gotten and the degree of fine-tuning you want.

1. Review the guiding questions and learning outcomes already entered into your design template. Ask yourself: Do my guiding questions set the stage for my learning outcomes? Do I have a logical flow from beginning to end? Have I allocated time appropriately?
2. Make adjustments to content and sequencing as needed.
3. Enter your standards/objectives and your ideas for activities, assessments, and resources into the template.

Evaluate Your Work

Your unit or course is probably sparkling by now. As a final step, assess your unit using the final unit checklist available on the book's website. The checklist reviews the principles and practices addressed throughout the entire book. And there we have it! You've reached the end of the journey.

Conclusion

Congratulations! You've done it: You've unleashed your creativity to reach your students more effectively and prepare them to topple the narrative that things can't change. You've gained a voice to call out inequities and the skills to make change through your curriculum.

As you move forward, remember that as educators, we always have a choice: We can teach content that helps students flourish or deprives them of vision. We can foster agency or model apathy. We can demonstrate respect or dismiss students with disdain. Our choices deeply matter because it all comes down to this: Students can write only the stories we teach.

References

Brookhart, S. M. (2011). Educational assessment knowledge and skills for teachers. *Educational Measurement: Issues and Practice, 30*(1), 3–12.

Wiggins, G. P., & McTighe, J. (2005). *Understanding by design* (2nd ed.). Alexandria, VA: Association for Supervision and Curriculum Development.

Wraga, W. G. (2010, August 18). Dangerous blind spots in the Common-Core standards. *Education Week*. Retrieved from https://www.edweek.org/ew/articles/2010/08/18/01wraga.h30.html?qs=common+core+narrows+the+curriculum

INDEX